Early P

THE MULTI-OF

MW00990999

"In a world where women are constantly faced with pressure to be or look a certain way, *The Multi-Orgasmic Diet* is like a breath of fresh air. Rebecca provides a playful, pleasurable, and loving approach to what is often full of shame and restriction. This book turns traditional dieting on its head and has the potential to help many women live ecstatic lives."

~Margot Anand, Founder of SkyDancing Tantra®
and Author of *The Art of Everyday Ecstasy*

"It's time for a complete revolution in the ways we've been conditioned to diet, deny and disrespect our bodies. Rebecca Gould shows us exactly how to wake up to the real source of our feminine power and start pleasuring rather than punishing ourselves so we can truly know our embodied radiance as women."

~ Lisa Schrader, Founder of Awakening Shakti

"Rebecca is a master at self-love. Her beautiful words are calming, steady and soft, much like a meditation as she weaves us through a journey of worthiness, strength, and comfort inside of our own skin. A type of 'diet' I'll take any day, any hour, over and over again."

~ Victoria Erickson, Author, *Edge of Wonder* and *Rhythms & Roads*

"The Multi-Orgasmic Diet is the first diet you will be able to stick to! It might change how you think about diets forever—and no green juice!"

~ Pamela Madsen, Founder of Back to The Body
Sensuous Retreats For Women

"Having grown up in France, in a culture that prizes pleasure and requires it as much as an every day multivitamin, I am deeply excited to see Rebecca's book reach many hands, many hearts, and many bodies. Her work has the power to create a delicious and essential shift in women's lives—which, of course, then carries over to simply . . . many lives."

~ Laura Lavigne, TEDx Speaker and Founder of
The Happiness Sprinkling Project

"Nurturing and nourishing your sexuality and sensuality is your birthright and essential to good self-care. Passionate about supporting women in coming into wholeness and living more joyful lives, Rebecca has given women a beautiful gift that will educate, awaken and inspire! *The Multi-Orgasmic Diet: Embrace Your Sexual Energy and Awaken Your Senses for a Healthier, Happier, Sexier You* will support you in living a juicier, more passion-filled life. I love this book!"

~ Renee Trudeau, Coach, Speaker, and Author of *The Mother's Guide to Self-Renewal: How to Reclaim, Rejuvenate and Re-Balance Your Life*

"Rebecca is a 'possibility realist.' She offers us the possibility to live a fuller, juicier life in a grounded way. She offers wisdom, humor and exercises that take into account our fears, doubt and self-judgments that, when not dealt with, sabotage our actions toward the life we want. Many of the practices Rebecca offers to help you move through those blockages are similar to what I share with my clients. They work! And I am excited to have this book to offer my clients!"

~ Jane Tornatore, PhD, LMFT

"Rebecca gracefully communicates the symbiotic relationship between living a full, rich, pleasure-filled life and a conscious, healthy relationship with food. This is no 'diet' book, but a recipe book with delicious ingredients that enrich daily life with orgasm in a way that nourishes and fulfills the hunger of your soul."

~ Yarah Sutra, The Pleasure Priestess of Unapologetically WOMAN

"Rebecca Clio Gould reveals how alive you can feel every day, when you live filling up on the pleasure of life. Her book is filled with deep wisdom and life-enhancing practices to help us be our healthiest, happiest, and sexiest selves—what fun! Rebecca's writing style is pure delight and I didn't want to put the book down."

~ Dhebi DeWitz, Author of *The Messenger Within*

"I got so excited reading Rebecca's *Multi-Orgasmic Diet* that I had to stop, fondle, and flirt with myself. You'll become a born again Pleasure Activist, delighting in how sexual energy and food can reshape your life! Feast on the fun and life-changing insights!"

~ Charla Hathaway, PhD, Sex & Intimacy Coach, Author of *Erotic Massage*, and Founder of BodyJoy Intimacy School

"In this world dominated by external authority figures attempting to undermine our authentic power, *The Multi-Orgasmic Diet* is a wise and precious antidote for reclaiming our receptive knowing. Filled with gentle, tender practices designed to awaken sensual living in every aspect of our lives, this book is a revolution in self-care and self-love."

~ Mellissae Lucia, Author and Creatrix of *The Oracle of Initiation*

THE
MULTI-
Orgasmic
DIET

Embrace Your Sexual Energy
and Awaken Your Senses for a
Healthier, Happier, Sexier You

REBECCA CLIO GOULD

ELEMENTAL HARMONY PRESS
2017

Published by Elemental Harmony Press
P.O. Box 33433
Seattle, WA 98133
www.themultiorgasmicdiet.com

Grateful acknowledgment is made to the following for permission to reprint previously published material:

The International Sheng Zhen Society: for permission to quote from *Awakening the Soul* (Master Li Junfeng © 2013), published by the International Sheng Zhen Society.

Kamala Chambers: for permission to quote from *Road to Love* (Kamala Chambers © 2014), published by Kamala Chambers.

Shakti Malan: for permission to quote from *Sexual Awakening for Women* (Dr. Shakti Mari Malan © 2012), published by SHAKTI.

Institute for Integrative Nutrition® and IIN® are trademarks of Integrative Nutrition Inc. Primary Food, Secondary Food and Crowding Out are IIN concepts © 2005 Integrative Nutrition Inc. (used with permission).

Notice: Mention of specific companies, organizations, or authorities in this book does not imply endorsement by the publisher, nor does mention of specific companies, organizations, or authorities imply that they endorse this book. Web addresses provided in this book were accurate at the time of publication.

The information contained in this book is intended to be educational and not for diagnosis, prescription, or treatment of any physical or mental health disorder whatsoever. This information should not replace consultation with a competent healthcare professional. The content in this book is intended to be used as an adjunct to a rational and responsible healthcare program prescribed by a professional healthcare practitioner. The author and publisher are in no way liable for any misuse of the material.

Design and composition by Sheila Parr
Cover design by Sheila Parr
Cover image © OlgaYakovenko / iStock
Author photo by Sharon Smith

ISBN: 978-0-9976645-0-8
eBook ISBN: 978-0-9976645-4-6

CONTENTS

Dedicated to all women.

Read This First

* Lost your mojo and yearning for a juicier, more fulfilling life?

* Tired of feeling bad about food, your body, or your general state of health?

* Sick of filling the void in ways that bring you down even more?

If you answered "yes" to any of these questions, then you have come to the right place. And if you've felt turned off in the past by diet books with all sorts of rules about what you can eat and how much to eat, don't worry. This, my friend, is not that type of diet book. Far from it.

The Multi-Orgasmic Diet is more than just a diet. **It's a way of being turned on by life so that you feel satisfied and fully alive.** Imagine living a life in which you feel excitement and find sensual pleasure in everything around you, as you delight in life's valleys and peaks. Living "turned on" in this way will give you more energy and sexual enjoyment. It will even help you slim down naturally and relatively effortlessly *if* that is one of your goals and what your body needs.

Where You're At Is Not Your Destiny

Maybe you've struggled with weight your entire life or have just recently started to put on the pounds. Perhaps you're a compulsive eater or someone who has always had to fight a sluggish metabolism. You might not even realize how readily these things tie into your sexuality, but they do. Your sex drive, your orgasms, how you see and feel about yourself—they're all related. No matter what you're dealing with, you're not alone, and there is hope. If you're ready to address these concerns with a sexy, fun, light-hearted approach, this book will help you feel your best, both in and out of the kitchen and in and out of the bedroom.

You'll find that the Multi-Orgasmic Diet will require *some* effort and dedication, but not in the same way as other diet books and health regimens. For example, instead of a menu plan full of foods to avoid and foods to eat, **you'll have a menu full of energy cultivation practices and sensual delights** to choose from. You'll discover how befriending your body, awakening your senses, and cultivating your life-force energy will enhance your pleasure potential and help you reach your health and wellness goals. The practices in this book will help you curb cravings and enjoy healthier foods and activities—all in a way that won't feel restrictive, shaming, or difficult to implement.

This isn't a bait and switch; this is thinking outside the box. This is about ending shame and taboos about food and sexuality by exploring the link between your eating habits or compulsions and your desire for love and connection. While *The Multi-Orgasmic Diet* won't teach you how to become orgasmic in the traditional sense of the word—that would be a book in and of itself—it will help you *feel* orgasmic and embrace sex and masturbation as healthy parts of self-care.

My Promise to You

This book will teach you how to start cultivating your sexual and vital life-force energy, so you'll experience more pleasure and success throughout your life. You'll awaken and engage your senses and connect more deeply with your world, your body, and your inner wisdom. By engaging more fully, you'll take control of your cravings and discover healthy ways to feed yourself and feel satisfied—both with and without food.

As for words like "orgasmic," "diet," and "sexy," they'll take on new meanings that you define. And whether you're partnered or single, sexually active or not, you'll learn to spice up your *whole* life with sexual energy, so that you can live turned on.

Sounds nice, right? Intriguing even? Perhaps you're wondering what living turned on means. So let me tell you. Living turned on means walking through life with an open heart and open mind, awakened senses, and more awareness of the vital life-force and sexual energy running through you. It means allowing yourself to feel more arousal, excitement, pleasure, and therefore fulfillment, all throughout your day.

And the reason this matters in terms of your diet? Too many of us are living dull lives and feeling down on ourselves for not being skinny enough, fit enough, or sexy enough. Not being good enough. Not living life to our fullest potential. Feeling an inexplicable emptiness. And then filling that void with junk—whether it be junk food, excessive social media, crappy TV shows, or unfulfilling relationships. I know this from the stories my clients and students share with me, and from personal experience.

This Is Personal for Me

For much of my life, I struggled with weight, body image, and loneliness. I certainly didn't feel turned on, at least not by life. I did often feel sexually aroused and even figured out how to orgasm and climax through masturbation at a young age. But I'm talking about something more than that, something beyond the genitals and the bedroom door. I lacked passion, connection, fulfillment, and pleasure in my life. So where did I turn for those things? I often turned to my best friends: Ben & Jerry. We'd sit on the couch watching a movie, and at first, the creamy sweetness of the ice cream felt good and soothing and delightful. But without fail, I'd wake up the next day feeling anxious, bloated, and filled with regret.

It wasn't until I discovered **energy cultivation practices and the power of self-love** that I began to feel a spark for life ignite in me. This was thanks to a form of heart-opening qigong you'll learn more about soon. But something was still missing. It wasn't until I also began studying conscious sexuality and practices to facilitate the awakening and deepening of my connection to my own feminine sexual essence that I truly started to *live turned on*.

I remember a friend sending me a newsletter promoting a course called Awakening Feminine Sexual Essence, taught by a world-renowned dakini (sacred sexuality teacher) named Shakti Malan, and I was intrigued. Soon I was learning from Shakti all about the importance of softening into my receptive feminine sexuality, entering more deeply into my body and heart, and opening up to my true sexual power.

I realized I'd been pushing myself too hard for years, operating mostly from the masculine energy within. I had been cut off from my feminine softness and receptivity, and this course helped me get in touch with the pleasure of being a woman.

Real Results, Real Pleasure

Without even trying, I began making healthier, less compulsive food choices. I wasn't "on a diet," and I wasn't trying to lose weight, yet people kept asking me if I was on a diet and telling me I looked great. Looking back on it now, I see I had slimmed down a bit, but mostly I was just happier, more energetic, more confident, and more satisfied, and therefore I was radiating a healthier glow. I'd like to help you experience the same kind of transformation in which you focus less on restriction and more on living it up.

The Link Between Sexuality, Anxiety, and Emotional Eating

You may be wondering what sexual energy and pleasure, an open heart, and awakened senses have to do with dieting. Let's start with this: food is often abused as an anti-anxiety drug. And guess what! Sexual pleasure, gratification, and expression can reduce and prevent anxiety. Isn't that great? **Cultivating your sexual energy and incorporating practices designed to bring more peace and pleasure into your life will help prevent and alleviate anxiety.** And that can prevent overeating and compulsive or emotional eating.

But there's more to this equation than sexual energy. Living turned on also requires an open heart and a connection with the energy of love. As psychologist Wilhelm Reich explains in *The Function of the Orgasm*, it's not just thwarted attempts at sexual gratification that lead to anxiety, but also thwarted attempts at love. Therefore, you'll be learning practices that not only engage your sexual pleasure centers but will also help you cultivate, feel, and express more love—for yourself, for others, and for life in general.

The Problem with Most Diets

Most diets feel too restrictive to induce a sense of living turned on, so they end up backfiring. Hence, we often experience the yo-yo effect. When I was a little girl, I was very overweight. I was put on diets and also witnessed my parents going on and off diets throughout my childhood. They never worked, at least not for the long term.

As I grew older, I became fascinated with nutrition from a Taoist and Traditional Chinese Medicine perspective. This fascination began after a nearly fatal car accident when I was sixteen. The injuries I sustained in the crash led to two-thirds of my intestines being removed. The doctors didn't know if I'd ever be able to eat or eliminate normally again. Fortunately, thanks to receiving a lot of Reiki (a form of energy work that can be done hands-on as well as from a distance), I had what doctors called a "miraculous" recovery. And after a few months of intravenous nutrition, I could eat and eliminate just fine. But I felt depressed and was gaining weight, and I didn't want to take anti-depressants. So I started studying the connection between food and mood to clean up my diet and alleviate my blues.

Although they once appealed to me, I don't believe in fad diets anymore. As for diets that *are* important for some people to follow (i.e., autoimmune or gluten-free), I see too many people approaching them in a way that's no fun. Why not approach them in a way that feels good, so you can enjoy the experience of making positive changes to your diet and lifestyle? It's also important to take the individual into account because we are all different and have unique dietary needs. Most diets out there will just lump you in with a group, though. Stick a label on you and tell you what to do. Am I right?

The Multi-Orgasmic Diet is not going to do that. I'm not going to label you or tell you exactly what to eat or what not to eat. Instead, I will guide you through learning how to truly **nourish and feed yourself not only with healthy whole foods and water, but with soul food, such as breath, touch, movement, and pleasure.** You'll learn to engage all of your senses and shift your mindset toward living a juicier life.

The Connection between Nourishment and Pleasure

Even if you are following a strict protocol, such as a gluten-free or auto-immune diet, I really want to empower you to tune in to your own body wisdom to identify your desires and needs. The practices in this book are designed to help you develop your ability to deeply connect with your body and inner wisdom. This will help you know what, when, and how to nourish and respect your body in a way that feels easy, honoring, and pleasurable rather than challenging, restrictive, and depressing. It *can* feel depressing and shaming when we think we can't or shouldn't eat a certain way. It can even feel like punishment, but the Multi-Orgasmic Diet can be used in conjunction with other diets to alleviate or prevent the negative experiences of restriction, boredom, and grief.

I wish for you to see food as an opportunity for self-love—self-*pleasuring* even—and in a healthy pleasure way rather than a guilty pleasure way. I want you to know how to fill yourself up with life, and then the actual food part will come easier.

Fuel for Living Fully Alive

My clients and students often tell me they wish they had more energy. Most people I know want more energy. They want to feel vibrant and happy and fully engaged with life. They want to feel they're living life to the fullest, and that requires having energy to go out and do those things that fill us up with even *more* energy.

And to do that we need food.

So if you want to live life to the fullest, it's important to consider the type of dietary fuel you're putting into your body as well as how you're fueling it. Although this book will not concentrate on nutrition per se, it will teach you ways in which you can make eating a fun, sensual delight rather than a chore that reeks of restriction, overindulgence, or guilt. But mostly you will learn how to boost your energy with non-food sources (that's the main focus here, after all), and there are plenty of practices throughout the book that are specifically designed to rev you up.

When you incorporate the Multi-Orgasmic Diet into your life and embark on this journey with clarity and commitment, and when you experience feeling fueled, filled up, and fed by *everything*, then you won't need that pint of ice cream, that beer after work, or that extra slice of pizza. You might choose to indulge and delight in such things at times, but you'll do so consciously and guilt-free rather than out of compulsion. And when you truly feel good and shame-free about what you're eating, you will be less likely to experience the aftershocks of physical dis-ease or emotional distress.

Sexy from the Inside Out

It's hard to feel sexy when you feel sick to your stomach from overindulgence or sick with worry because of food or body image issues. And I'm guessing one reason you picked up this book is because you want to feel sexier, right? Or even just *sexy*—forget the "er" for now. Whether they realize it or not, most women I know want to feel sexy. We often think of "sexy" as how someone looks and behaves, and these looks and behaviors are usually encouraged and even dictated by the media. What we see in the media is rarely *truly* sexy, though.

What's truly sexy is having the courage to live turned on, to show up in each moment as your authentic self, and to exude a sense of confidence, lusciousness, and playfulness. And all of that comes from within and is intrinsically linked to your sexuality. So who cares if you're slim or curvy, have short or long hair, like makeup or not, wear skirts or sweats? What matters is how you feel on the inside. And I want to help you *feel* super sexy because I know that you will then *look* sexier, *feel* better, and *live* a happier life.

Nerves Are Normal

If you're ready for a change, to live turned on, and to see your body, mind, and spirit transform into the healthiest version of you, whatever size or shape that may be, then *The Multi-Orgasmic Diet* is for you. Sound good? Or does some of this sound a bit scary to you?

If you feel some hesitation, fear, and discomfort, don't worry. Part of what this book does is help you face your fears so that you can move through them and beyond them to experience a sense of exhilaration and liberation. Using this book might be all it takes to help you deal with any fear or resistance bubbling up, but you also might need additional support, whether from a coach like me, a psychotherapist, a Somato-Emotional Release (SER) therapist, or some other wellness professional.

So are you ready to feel sexy from the inside out? Are you ready for that inner sex appeal to start radiating out into the world? Sexual power is your birthright, and *The Multi-Orgasmic Diet* will help you tap into that by teaching you to unleash your feminine power and enjoy life more. When you do, you'll feel fulfilled and less stressed, which equates to less emotional eating, less tension, and less holding on to excess fat or things that just don't serve you.

I invite you now to go beyond your comfort zone and **empower yourself through self-knowledge, self-love, and pleasure.** Claim your right to live large and be fulfilled, sexually and otherwise.

"Your pleasure heals the world."

~YARAH SUTRA, THE PLEASURE
PRIESTESS

Redefining Multi-Orgasmic: Some Key Terms and How I Use Them

There is no need to memorize these terms, but reading them now may be useful, and you can refer back to them later if needed:

Multi-orgasmic: the ability to *live turned on* and experience multiple instances of unrestrained, intense excitement and joy as you feel the pleasure of energy flowing through you, whether overtly sexual or not. This definition is elaborated upon throughout the book. By engaging in the practices, you will learn what it truly means.

Living turned on: a metaphor for walking through life with an open heart and open mind, awakened senses, and more awareness of the vital life-force and sexual energy running through you. Living turned on means allowing yourself to feel more arousal, excitement, pleasure, and therefore fulfillment, all throughout your day, all throughout your life.

Diet: the kinds of *soul food* in which you habitually partake. *The Multi-Orgasmic Diet* is primarily about the ways in which you nourish your soul and feed yourself energetically and sensually, rather than the particular foods you choose to eat. And you will discover how cultivating sexual energy and awakening the senses lead to making healthier food choices without the sense of restriction found in standard diets.

Vital Life-force Energy, or Qi *(sounds like "chee")*: the energy that sustains life and is in all living things. In Chinese, this energy is called qi and is sometimes spelled "chi." If you are familiar with the yogic term "prana," it is basically the same thing.

Sexual Energy: our *creative* life-force energy. Although a powerful energy that does not always have to do with sexual *arousal*, "sexual energy" is primarily used in this context for its ability to spark feelings of passion, exhilaration, and pleasure. I use the terms "sexual energy" and "orgasmic energy" throughout the book, and while they have subtle differences in meaning, their core idea is the same.

Qigong *(sounds like "chee gung")*: an ancient process of exchanging qi with the Universe through movement, breath, and intention for greater health and well-being.

Sheng Zhen and Sheng Zhen Gong *(sounds like "shung jen" and "shung jen gung")*: Sheng Zhen means Unconditional Love. Sheng Zhen Gong is the *practice* of cultivating Unconditional Love using various forms of movement. It has a unique focus on opening the heart and cultivating the pure, universal energy of love along with qi. Having a Sheng Zhen practice is good for physical health, balances the emotions, and elevates the spirit.

Cultivating energy vs. Harnessing energy: Cultivating energy refers to acquiring more and/or strengthening your energy in preparation for use, while harnessing energy refers to controlling and making use of it in a conscious way that actually produces even more energy. In the process of cultivating and harnessing your sexual energy, you may, in fact, be "awakening" this force within you for the first time in your life. Cultivation also refers to the ongoing and deepening *practice* of something, such as opening the heart or awakening the senses.

Yoni: Yoni literally means "cave" or "sacred space" and is the Sanskrit term for vulva, vagina, and womb. It is regarded as a symbol of divine procreative power, a symbol of Shakti, the female principle of divine energy.

How to Use this Book

This book is meant to be a guide you can utilize, as well as a fun and easy read. Many other books addressing sexuality or diet are either too serious or too advanced, too intimidating or too esoteric, or they lack depth, heart, and soul. This book is meant to be a gateway into deeper self-cultivation practices, while also providing effective and low-stress methods for eating healthier and living a more active, joyful, pleasure-filled life.

So here's what you're going to do. Instead of counting calories, you'll be counting your blessings and your breaths. Instead of cutting out fat or carbs, you'll be cutting out self-sabotaging, self-shaming thoughts and behaviors. Instead of adding in supplements, you'll be adding in orgasms and self-pleasuring sessions. And have no fear if you have difficulty with orgasm and pleasure, or even if those words make you feel uncomfortable or squeamish; this book will help with that, too.

That's right. This is no old-school diet book or fad diet. Instead of being rigid and restrictive, you're going to get more in touch with your body and with what brings you pleasure and joy. You will learn what leads you to make unhealthy as well as healthy choices as *The Multi-Orgasmic Diet* shows you how to unleash and tap into your sexual energy. As you do, you'll enhance your pleasure potential by slowing down and relaxing into living life to the fullest. You'll even discover how to feel fulfilled without overeating or emotional eating as well as how to feel less shame and more joy even when you do occasionally overindulge.

Set Your Own Course

You can read through this book at any pace, though I encourage you to digest it in small, bite-sized morsels. Slowing down and taking time, in general, is part of the journey and the process. Giving yourself time and space to incorporate these practices into your life will help you benefit more fully from them. Rather than rushing to cram it all in or get to the end goal overnight, consider taking it slow.

Aim to focus on at least one chapter per week. Even if you devour the book quickly, keep it out and available as a reference, so that every day, or week, you can select new practices to incorporate and layer into your "diet."

I'm a big fan of choose-your-own-adventure, so you can go at your own pace, layering in one practice at a time or following a full menu plan from the beginning. You can create your own way of incorporating the practices and suggestions in this book, or you can follow the sample menu plans found in chapter 12. How you choose to use the information given to you here depends on your goals, motivations, and personal preferences.

Make Your Commitment Real

I do ask that you commit to taking this journey because there is great power in commitment. For optimal results, engage in at least one of the forthcoming practices prior to a meal, or at every meal, and before or instead of snacking.

While it's true that simply reading this book can give you some subtle or short-term change, for the most noticeable and sustainable changes, it is crucial to put this knowledge into action. There is no magic pill. Developing daily practices and taking consistent actions over time will be most beneficial. Results may come quickly and be big, or they may come slowly, start off small, and grow over time. Or some combination of the two. **There's no right or wrong here—just consistent steps to follow.**

It's also important to have sincere intention and focus, but don't be too serious or rigid. Being relaxed helps your sexual energy flow, and it can also help you lose weight if that's one of your needs. When your body feels stressed, it holds on to fat, but when it's relaxed, it lets go more easily. Plus, when you're relaxed and energy is flowing, blood flow is better (which is also essential for sexual arousal), and that means your circulation and metabolism can burn calories and fat, and also flush out toxins, more efficiently.

A Note Regarding Weight Loss

The Multi-Orgasmic Diet is not a weight loss program per se, but weight loss *may* occur. If you need to lose a lot of weight for health reasons, then this book alone may not be the best approach; it might be more of a fun, supportive supplement while you adhere to some other diet plan or work with a weight loss specialist. If you're just trying to lose five to ten pounds or drop a pants size or two, no *promise* here. However, weight loss and slimming down are likely to occur along with living a more active lifestyle, feeling more fulfilled, and making more loving and conscious choices.

There are lots of reasons people gain weight or can't seem to lose weight. Sometimes the pressure of losing weight or looking a certain way can be a powerful motivator, but more often than not, it's self-defeating and contributes to feelings of inadequacy, something being wrong with you, and increased anxiety.

When you stop restricting yourself and start getting into a healthier relationship with yourself and your body, it will be easier to slim down or to realize there's no need to focus on trying to. For example, one of my clients came to me wanting to drop at least fifty pounds. But after experiencing some personal transformation in which her heart opened, she was no longer so concerned about losing weight. Her excess weight had been holding her back from going out and being more active. But once she felt her heart opening up, she filled with joy and could go out into the world and enjoy it regardless of her size. And as a consequence? Her compulsive eating decreased, and so did the numbers on the scale.

So unless you really need to for health reasons (in which case, consult a doctor), I encourage you *not* to be so hung up on losing weight. Instead, **put your energy into enjoying life, opening your heart, and loving and pleasuring yourself.** This will lead to sustainable changes in which weight loss may just be a bonus. Alternatively, if you actually need to *gain* weight, the same thing applies. The more you love yourself and enjoy life, and the more in touch with your body and inner wisdom you are, the easier it will be to eat more of the foods your body needs in order to be at its healthiest weight, shape, and size.

So ditch the scale and the measuring tape. Don't get caught up in numbers, pounds, and measurements. Instead, get caught up in the ecstasy of life. Get swept away by bliss while also being present in each pleasurable moment after pleasurable moment. Pay more attention to how you feel than how you look. The more you focus on feeling good, the more that goodness will radiate out as a sexy glow, and the more you will make the best, healthiest food and exercise choices for yourself. This is what living turned on and *The Multi-Orgasmic Diet* are all about.

Chapter 1

SETTING YOURSELF UP
FOR SUCCESS

"Until one is committed, there is hesitancy,
the chance to draw back."

~ W. H. MURRAY

Welcome to Chapter One. I can only imagine how eager you must be to dive into the juicy stuff (and believe me, it's here). But how many times have you started reading a book or tried a new program without finishing or getting the results you wanted? I don't want that to happen to you here. So now that you have some background on my motivation for writing this book, it's time to start laying a foundation for your success. This chapter will help you clarify your goals and show you how to commit to them. You'll also learn how to make time for the practices that will help you live a multi-orgasmic life.

One of the biggest barriers to developing healthy habits and achieving sustainable transformation is the excuse of not having enough time—or being too tired or "not feeling like it." How often has something—like adding in a meditation practice or going to the gym—just seemed too hard to fit into your schedule or like too much work? Although I offer a variety of short and easy practices designed to fit easily into your life, boost your energy, and help you "feel like it," you will experience optimal benefit by looking at time management and the fine art of slowing down. It's important to lay this groundwork and be patient with the process as it unfolds.

First things first, though. What do you want? And why? Why are you even reading this book? To what are you willing and able to commit?

Get out a pen and a journal. If you don't have a journal, use a piece of paper, but I recommend you get a notebook to use as a journal. Dedicate it to your commitment to live a turned-on, orgasmic life. And then? Continue.

Clarifying Goals

Before going any further, you need to know where you'd like to end up. Maybe the answer is already crystal clear, or maybe it requires some digging. You might need to consider some questions, such as:

- What's most important to me? What do I want?
- Do I want to have more energy?
- Do I want to lose ten pounds? Do I just want to fit into my jeans better?
- Do I want to look and feel more attractive and vibrant?
- Do I want to stop compulsive or emotional eating?
- Do I want to feel more luscious and experience more pleasure?
- Do I want to be able to enjoy a freakin' piece of cake without guilt?

It doesn't matter if you pick something on this list or fill in the blanks for yourself. What counts is making a choice that's right for you. However, even if your goal is to lose ten pounds or look a certain way, I suggest focusing more on how you want to *feel*.

Allow me to explain. My good friend and colleague Laura Lavigne teaches about the importance of focusing on Essence rather than Form. And that's what I invite you to do here. Let's say you want to lose ten pounds. That's the Form. But to get to the Essence, you first must ask,

Why? What will that do for me? How will that make me feel? Some possible answers for what the long-term payoff will feel like are:

- Health
- Joy
- Confidence
- Accomplishment
- Sexiness

You get the point? When you focus more on those feelings—that Essence—you're likely to get results faster. You'll feel better sooner regardless of what the scale says or what size you want to be. Don't believe me? Start practicing, give it time, and see what happens.

Practice:

ESSENTIAL GOALS & DESIRED OUTCOMES

Step 1. For each of these time periods—1 month, 3 months, and 6 months—answer the following questions to clarify your goals:

1. What do I want?
2. What will that do for me?
3. How will that make me feel?

Although this could be applied to various aspects of your life, such as career or relationships, start off with whatever feels most relevant to why you even purchased this book. Was it because you don't like what you see when you look in the mirror? Was it because your life feels lackluster? Or because you wanted to lose weight? Feel sexier? Get in better shape?

What do you want? What will that do for you or get you? And how will that make you feel? Ask yourself these questions often, and repeat as needed.

Selecting the Essence words for your goals and writing them out on cards to keep in sight is helpful too, and Laura Lavigne even has a deck of Essence cards you can find online (see Resources for a link).

Step 2. Focus on these Essence words throughout your day, every day. Notice when and where you experience these feelings, regardless of the form. Notice yourself moving more toward what and who brings about these feelings in you.

Now that it's clear where you want to go, what are you willing to do to get there? The most basic, foundational answer here is commit. Commit and engage with the practices in this book on a regular basis. There will be times that your resistance, impatience, doubts, and your inner critic or old habits will try to stop you, so in the next section, let's shine light on those dark places. Let's bring awareness to what might get in your way as well as to what you have going for you.

Handling Roadblocks

Identifying your strengths and weaknesses will help prepare you for the roadblocks and hiccups that might arise while on the path to a more joyous life. This will increase the likelihood of continuing to move forward to reach your goals instead of giving up along the way.

Practice:

IDENTIFYING STRENGTHS & WEAKNESSES

You can make a list of words, write full sentences, or even compose paragraphs. Just write whatever comes; you can always add to it or make changes later.

My greatest weaknesses are (list at least 3):
For example, *ice cream, self-doubt, and impatience—I have a hard time sticking with something long enough to see the results I want.*

My greatest strengths are (list at least 5):
For example, *finding silver linings, my sense of humor, I'm a good listener, willing to try new things, my smile.*

Voila! You are now more prepared to draw on your strengths to handle those weaknesses. How so? Let's take my example. Knowing that I have a weakness for ice cream, I can draw on my strength of humor to not be hard on myself if I give in to an ice cream craving. Or I can draw on my strength of willingness to try new things to come up with something other than ice cream to satisfy me. And knowing in advance that impatience is likely to arise, I can remind myself to give it time. I can also take note of what practices in my toolbox—or this book—could help me in times of impatience, self-doubt, or ice cream cravings. Make sense? I hope so. I want you to know that you have what it takes to succeed, to face your struggles in a loving and gentle way.

On a related note, there's something else to keep in check so that you have a smoother ride here: the inner critic and the inner saboteur. Because of the intimate nature of this book and the practices I'll be sharing with you, it's likely that some deep, dark, uncomfortable stuff could get stirred up.

You may be noticing little voices in your head that are criticizing you or this book or both, maybe even telling you not to bother. The inner critic and inner saboteur might already be rearing their ugly heads. Self-criticism and self-sabotage are forms of resistance that cause contraction, block your energy flow, and dim your light. To stop or minimize their damage, it's helpful to look at the ways in which you criticize and sabotage yourself.

Some say the saboteur and critic are the same thing. I say the inner saboteur is a close cousin of the inner critic. The critic feeds you all those nasty, judgmental thoughts about yourself, all those lies that keep you small, hold you back, and perpetuate your suffering. The saboteur tells you to do things that aren't really best for you or tells you *not* to do things that *are* best for you. Both speak up out of fear and resistance to positive change.

When the critic and saboteur show up, it's important to get out of your head and into your body. There will be plenty of practices in the coming pages to help you with that, with *embodiment*. But for now, you can just become more aware of their presence.

Practice:

CALLING OUT THE INNER CRITIC

1. If nothing's coming up for you in this moment, great! But if you already hear that nasty voice creeping in or can recall ways in which it has in the past, write it out. Get out your journal and a pen, and brain-dump your doubts, skepticism, and criticism. Sometimes you'll hear the critic in the first person, sometimes in the second person. For example, *This isn't going to work. Nothing ever does. I can't do this. You're not good enough. You always give up. This is stupid.*

2. When this voice comes up, say, "Hey, stop that. Leave me alone." Or engage in some witty banter with it and then tell it to fuck off. Seriously! It works. Another approach is to send it on vacation. Or kill it with kindness through the self-love practices you'll find in this book.

Recognizing the inner critic and learning how to not let it get to you will serve you well, as you progress through this book and in all aspects of life. The above practices can also work with the inner saboteur, but here are a couple of other approaches. Experiment with what works best for you.

Practice:

SEDUCING THE SABOTEUR

1. First, prepare for the seduction by getting more familiar. Make a list of the ways you sabotage yourself. For example, *I deny myself dessert when out with friends but then end up binging on ice cream when all alone.* Or, *I take on too much, leaving me feeling too depleted, drained,*

and busy for fun social opportunities. Or, I bought this book, but I'm not doing the practices.

2. Your inner saboteur wants attention and is afraid of change. Have a conversation with her. Sit or lie down somewhere comfortable. Shut your eyes to turn your attention more inward, breathe, and ask her what she really wants for you. And then? Listen. Most likely, she wants to feel good. Talk to her about the ways in which she'll benefit from leaving you alone.

Visit www.rebeccacliogould.com/bookbonus for a guided "Seducing the Saboteur" meditation. You may even discover your inner saboteur is a "he"!

There's no quick fix for fully eliminating those havoc-wreaking voices, but by implementing these practices, the voices will come less often and with less impact. It can be as easy as sending the critic and saboteur off on vacation together. Tell them to go have a play date with each other while you go play with yourself.

Speaking of playing with yourself, if you're wondering when we're going to get to that, be patient. We're getting there. Slowly, but surely. Enjoy this foreplay. In the next chapter, you'll begin learning how to play with your energy. But first, just like any worthwhile endeavor, there's still some preparation to do.

Making a Commitment

As the sayings go, "awareness is the first step" and "knowledge is power." However, neither awareness nor knowledge will do you much good if you don't put them to use. For success and sustainable results, you must commit to taking consistent actions. And no matter what your lifestyle, no matter what your routine or schedule is, you *can* do this, and you *will* make time for this *if* it's something you truly want. If you're ready and want it badly enough, then nothing will stop you. Plus, you get to set the pace here.

Now that you've identified what you want and why, what your strengths and weaknesses are, and how to handle those nasty voices inside, it's time to officially commit to your personal transformation by signing the general contract below. You can also find this online as one of your book bonuses at www.rebeccacliogould.com/bookbonus. You may edit it to suit your own needs, both in terms of what you're committing to and the way in which you word it. I highly recommend you give this a *minimum* of sixty-six days, and ideally ninety days or more, because it takes an average of sixty-six days to ingrain a new habit. If you don't have a printer, just get out a piece of paper or a 4x6 index card and write the following:

I, _____, hereby commit to the Multi-Orgasmic Diet. I commit to taking daily action and making a conscious choice to live my life more fully alive. I commit to getting more in touch with my body and my sexual energy, and awakening my senses so that I will feel more pleasure and fulfillment throughout my day and make healthier choices in all I do. I commit to focusing on pleasure, fun, and experimentation and keeping an open mind and a sense of curiosity, playfulness, and ease. I intend to give this *at least* 66 days, as I understand it takes time for real change and transformation to occur.

Signed: _____ Dated: _____

Congratulations! You are now committed. Remember, there is great power in commitment. Keep this contract somewhere where it is easy to refer to daily. Looking at it when you first wake up in the morning and before you go to sleep at night will help turbo-boost your experience. And since commitments and contracts have been known to work wonders, you also can sign more specific contracts as you progress through this book. For example, one practice I suggest incorporating as soon as you're ready is the Orgasmic Breath; you can find this in chapter 6. A sample contract for this practice follows:

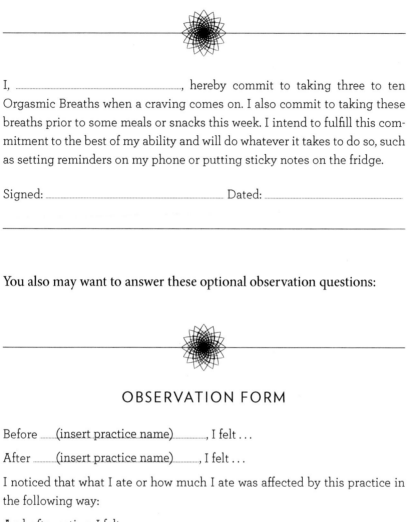

I, _____, hereby commit to taking three to ten Orgasmic Breaths when a craving comes on. I also commit to taking these breaths prior to some meals or snacks this week. I intend to fulfill this commitment to the best of my ability and will do whatever it takes to do so, such as setting reminders on my phone or putting sticky notes on the fridge.

Signed: _____ Dated: _____

You also may want to answer these optional observation questions:

OBSERVATION FORM

Before _____(insert practice name)_____, I felt . . .

After _____(insert practice name)_____, I felt . . .

I noticed that what I ate or how much I ate was affected by this practice in the following way:

And *after* eating, I felt . . .

Additional notes:

_____

_____

_____

An online editable version of this form is available at www.rebeccacliogould.com/bookbonus *and is suitable for any practice.*

These contracts and observation forms will help you stay focused and clear. The more you write, speak, or simply think about and visualize yourself living the way you want and doing what you say you're going to do, the more likely you are to succeed. I've seen it work wonders in my own life as well as in the lives of my clients and students. Many things can distract us from our mission in our daily lives, or we might lose steam or interest over time, but looking at our goals and commitments on a daily basis helps keep us focused and on track. Scheduling practices into your calendar, with alerts or alarms to remind you, will be helpful, too.

Time Management

Although some of the Multi-Orgasmic Diet menu items, a.k.a. *practices*, are short 'n' sweet or designed to be easily incorporated into other daily activities, it will greatly benefit you to carve out some extra time in order to achieve a positive, impactful experience from this book. As cliché as it sounds, this will allow you to stop and smell the roses, both literally and metaphorically.

How on earth will you do this? How will you find more time for things like longer meal breaks, self-pleasuring sessions, and other daily practices without ending up rushing around and feeling even more stressed out?

Relax. First of all, you're in control of how much or how little you incorporate the Multi-Orgasmic Diet into your life. Second, you may think you don't have time, but you do. You really do have all the time in the world for the things that matter most to you. It just might require making some changes, especially to your beliefs about time and priorities. And the first key to better time management? Take inventory of time wasters, time sucks, and energy drains as well as areas of your life that might need more time.

Practice:

FINDING THE TIME

Identify activities that are eating up more time than necessary and activities that aren't being given enough time. Whatever comes to mind is fine. You may also refer to the list below:

- Facebook or other social media
- checking email
- talking on the phone
- texting
- watching TV
- commuting
- cooking/meal prep
- eating
- yard work

- house cleaning
- business admin (if self-employed)
- work
- daydreaming
- reading
- meditation
- self-care
- sleep
- socializing

- hobbies
- grooming
- networking
- childcare
- time with friends
- time with lover or dating
- time with family
- alone time
- exercise

QUESTIONS TO CONTEMPLATE:

What is taking up too much time?
What's not getting enough time?
Where could I be more efficient?

Where can you shave off some minutes, or even a whole hour or more, to make time for the areas that aren't getting enough time, for the practices and action steps within this book, and for other activities and people in your life?

Tip: You may want to revisit this practice again as the week goes on, or even over the months. Just keep assessing where you can cut things out that are robbing you of the time and energy for those activities and people that matter most.

You don't necessarily need to *completely* cut out the time wasters and energy drains on your list, but if the total is considerable and keeping you from what matters most (i.e., *you*, your health and wellness goals, fostering fun and healthy relationships, etc.), then reprioritizing will help. For example, if you're hooked on some TV shows, try watching them while you work out or with friends as a social activity. As for checking email and social media, consider having a set amount of time each day or designated times to check those things. And if simply looking at this as *prioritizing* doesn't work for you, feel free to let these activities be like your *reward* for things like working out, prepping a healthy meal, or completing a practice from this book.

Also, consider silencing your phone more often and turning off notifications if you have a smartphone. Studies show that whether you realize it or not, all those distractions throughout the day add up and can make you feel less focused and less efficient. Device addiction or overuse also can affect the quality, or lack thereof, of your relationships with others as well as with yourself. Yes, Facebook and other online forms of entertainment and interaction can be a great source of pleasure, but make sure they're not getting in the way of something else. Certainly there's a way to balance enjoying the perks of being connected through technology with the importance of real live face-to-face interactions as well as device-free alone time. And finding that balance, whatever a healthy balance is for you, will help you feel as if you're living life to the fullest.

The Feminine Art of Slowing Down

Now that you've committed and considered how to free up some more time for yourself, you are ready for the next step in living a more sensual, pleasure-filled life: *slowing down*—a key component of connecting more deeply with your feminine sexual essence as well as a stress reliever and awareness enhancer. When you are more in touch with your femininity and sexuality, and walk through life in a relaxed state of heightened awareness, you are likely to experience more enjoyment and pleasure in life as well as the capacity to make healthier choices.

Most people spend their lives rushing to their graves. What are *you* rushing for? Rushing increases stress, thereby elevating cortisol (the stress hormone) and depleting oxytocin (known as the love or cuddle hormone). When the body is stressed, it's more likely to not only crave unhealthy foods but also to hold on to fat as part of a deeply ingrained survival mechanism. Also, although sometimes a sense of time pressure may be a turn-on during masturbation or sex, rushing usually takes away from your ability to experience optimal pleasure, or even minimal pleasure, during daily activities.

Consider this in terms of an everyday activity like driving. And if you don't drive, think of riding the bus, riding your bike, or walking instead. If you're rushing to get to an appointment and end up in traffic, instead of luxuriating in a leisurely drive and enjoying a book or a walk if you arrive early, you're sitting in traffic feeling agitated, unable to do anything about being stuck, and getting upset about the possibility or certainty of being late. Your breathing is shallow, your body is tense, and you're not happy.

Now imagine instead giving yourself an extra ten to twenty minutes, or even more, to get to wherever you're going. Don't worry right now about how that's even possible. **Just imagine.** Imagine leaving early and having plenty of time. It doesn't matter if there's unexpected traffic. You can enjoy some music or catch up with a friend on the phone while you drive. And if you arrive early, you can meditate, go for a walk, journal, or read. You're going to feel happier and more peaceful, breathe more fully, and feel better able to relax into the softness of your femininity—all of which are crucial to living a multi-orgasmic life.

I invite you to start experiencing the lusciousness of having more time, of not rushing. To do this might feel uncomfortable and even *impossible* and stressful at first, like you're cutting into work or some other project to have more time to eat and drive, or like there's no way that you *can*. But you can, and you will, and you must. As you saw in the time management section, it's possible to shave off a few minutes here or there from various activities so that you have more time.

Revisit the previous practice "Finding the Time" if needed. And then start playing around with "The Gift of Time," which follows.

Practice:

THE GIFT OF TIME

First, it's important to commit to yourself that you're going to *experiment* with giving yourself more time. Set boundaries in terms of your availability to others so that you have sufficient time for you.

And set alarms—schedule in reminders to pop up on your phone or computer telling you to leave earlier. If you usually take twenty to thirty minutes to get somewhere, leave ten minutes earlier.

Think about how you want to enjoy that commute, such as with music or catching up on the phone or simply enjoying some silence and taking in the scenery.

Also, consider how you are going to reward yourself if you arrive at your destination early. With a book? A catnap? A walk around the block? Or maybe a latte or a piece of chocolate? Yes, that's right—in the Multi-Orgasmic Diet, you can treat yourself to foods and drinks that other diet books would tell you to avoid, at least for now, because for now the focus is on pleasure and fun and awareness, not on rules about which foods to eat or avoid.

Tip: Consider keeping a journal or book in your car so that you always have a way to make the most of your time while also giving yourself the gift of more time to get where you're going.

As you begin creating space for the practices in this book, the best ones to start off with may be those that are easily incorporated into other daily activities and take only a few minutes. For example, when driving, let the horizon come to you. This idea was first introduced to me by Suzanne Scurlock-Durana when I attended her *Healing the Pelvic Floor* workshop at the Esalen Institute in 2009. She shared that her tai chi teacher said that when she drives long distances, she never feels depleted or tired because she allows the horizon to come to her. The following practice will explain this in more detail.

Practice:

LET THE HORIZON COME TO YOU

The next time you're driving, notice if your body is leaning forward a bit or if you feel a subtle energetic pull forward. And is your mind already at your destination? Or elsewhere? Come back into the moment and into your body.

Sink down deep inside. Take a deep breath. Relax. Drink in the scenery through your eyes. Let the horizon come to you. You will get where you're going; it doesn't require a big effort or energy expenditure.

Notice how this affects your mood and energy level. Do you feel more in touch with your feminine softness and receptivity?

Tip: You can also use the above technique to help yourself relax if you have not implemented the previous practice of gifting yourself more time and are concerned about running late. Remember that there's nothing you can do about the traffic. So you might as well surrender and enjoy the ride—as in all of life.

I use this technique eighty to ninety percent of the time now. Sometimes I forget, but the instant I remember, I also remember why it's so much better to take this approach. Why? Because I immediately notice my body and mind softening and a smile forming. I feel more at peace. More joyful. It feels like the relief of a break in the midst of all the things I feel I'm *striving* for. I can just let the road come to me, and that allows my energy to flow better, which helps me get more in touch with my pleasure potential and the sexual energy running through me. Now it's easier to feel turned on by all of life, even in the midst of traffic.

You still might be wondering, "What does any of this driving stuff have to do with food and diet and being my healthiest and sexiest self?" It's that connection to stress and anxiety. Remember? When you learn how to manage and reduce stress and anxiety, how to lean back, take it easy, and enjoy life more, you'll feel healthier and happier; your body will more easily let go of excess fat, your skin will glow, and you'll stop self-medicating with food. You will simply feel better about your life and about yourself, and *that* is healthy *and* sexy.

Accountability and the Importance of a Support System

We've covered a lot of the basics of setting yourself up for success. But there's one more thing: having support and accountability systems in place. My clients always say that *accountability* is one of the things they value most in working with a coach to reach their goals. From my experiences, both as a client and as a coach, I strongly agree. Having at least one friend or family member on board can be extremely helpful, too.

Some people, however, have some sort of negative connotation about the concept of "accountability." I assure you that it's not about punishment for not doing something; it's about helping you and holding you, a touchstone of sorts as you move through the process of transformation.

So how will you hold yourself accountable in a way that doesn't feel harsh or like pressure? Are there people around who will support you in making these lifestyle and dietary changes? Will telling someone else what you're doing actually help you follow through? Can you tell any of the people closest to you what you're up to? Maybe even invite them to take this journey along with you?

In addition to the general contract and practice-specific contracts, consider telling those close to you that you're making some changes. Let them know how they can support and respect you during this time, especially in the beginning as you're learning to make these diet and lifestyle changes. Perhaps you don't know yet how they can be supportive; in that case, start by simply telling them. That might be all it takes.

You can also join the MOD Facebook group to help you stay on track and meet like-minded women. And for additional support, individual or group coaching is a turbocharged way of going through this process. See the Resources section and Appendix 3 for details and other ideas.

Practice:

SUPPORT SYSTEM

List the people or the person you can talk to about this. If you feel shy or embarrassed, that's okay. In person or over the phone, you can start off by saying that. Be vulnerable. Or maybe you currently don't have anyone in your life you feel comfortable telling. In that case, or even if you do have people, I encourage you to turn to yourself and to your journal; be your own best friend and confidant.

You may also want to explore the following questions in your journal: *What sort of support do I want and need? What will help me succeed?* If you're not sure, just keep asking yourself and see what answers bubble up.

Bon Voyage!

In light of completing this chapter, you are now better prepared to embark on this journey, which means you're more likely to stick with it, enjoy it, get results, and make sustainable changes! Sometimes the hardest part of reaching our goals is getting started. But sometimes it's more about continuing and riding it out for long enough to see lasting results. Although you may experience changes right away, remember that this is not meant to be a quick fix. *The Multi-Orgasmic Diet* is about having fun getting really intimate with yourself physically, emotionally, and energetically while also learning how to treat yourself like your favorite lover so that you feel so happy, vibrant, and sexy that making healthy food and activity choices comes naturally.

IF YOU HAVEN'T ALREADY, go back and identify your goals and sign that contract. Then start playing around with the driving practices. Even something as simple as letting the horizon come to you can make a big difference in your life and requires no additional time or scheduling.

Remember to access your book bonuses at www.rebeccacliogould.com/bookbonus.

Chapter 2

WHAT THE HECK IS ENERGY, AND WHY DOES IT MATTER?

"Sexual energy is life-force energy. You can't stifle it without consequences: be they health problems ranging from excess weight, to reproductive ailments, to emotional issues like depression and excess anger, to the breakdown of a marriage. If you aren't tapping into that energy, I guarantee that parts of your life are stagnating."

~ KIM ANAMI

How would you like to have more energy and the know-how to tap into, direct, and amplify it? Imagine if, rather than feeling drained and lethargic or unmotivated, you could feel more awake, sexually vibrant, and animated . . . *without* needing a cup of coffee or a sugary treat? Imagine actually having the energy and drive to go out and live your life in a way that would fill you up with even more energy, vitality, and pleasure.

Most people view food—or even coffee—as a primary energy source, but there is a pure form of energy inside of you that isn't solely derived from food. This energy is also all around you in an infinite supply. It is known as qi (pronounced "chee"), which is Chinese for vital life-force energy.

One of my main intentions with this book is to help you discover your potential to live more fully alive by tapping into this life-force energy and, more specifically, your sexual energy. Why? Because it will help you feel like the goddess that you are, empowered and confident and better able to choose foods and activities that are nourishing and healing rather than harmful and depleting. Understanding and cultivating this non-food source of energy is foundational to the Multi-Orgasmic Diet. And by increasing your awareness of it, you can heighten your sensitivity and increase your ability to *feel* this energy, which will empower you, energize you, and increase your capacity for arousal and pleasure.

So what exactly *is* this energy? Keep reading to find out . . .

Qi ~ Vital Life-Force Energy

Every living thing has qi. You're born with it, and it's in the air you breathe and even the food you eat. The literal translation of "qi" is "breath, air, or gas," but figuratively, qi is "energy." And it's a different type of energy than when someone speaks of the "energy" of a house or a place or any inanimate object. It's not the kind of electric energy that would turn on a light bulb. **Qi sustains living things.** It is sometimes described as the pulsation of the cosmos itself. But what the heck does that mean? Feel it for yourself:

Practice:

FEEL THE QI

1. Sit comfortably at the edge of your chair (or sit all the way back if needed) with your spine straight and hands resting on your lap, palms facing up. Close your eyes.

2. Bring your attention to your feet and feel that they create a stable support in addition to the chair. Sense the ground through your feet and imagine you are sending roots down into the earth. This will help you feel focused and calm and connected to the earth; this will help you feel *grounded*.

3. Breathe naturally. Breathe consciously—think about effortlessly breathing in fresh, pure healing energy and sending out stagnant, murky energy. Notice your breath slowing down, and feel your body relaxing as you breathe.

4. Feel as if your hands are huge. Just focus on the palms of your hands, and then bring your hands into prayer position: left palm and right palm come together in front of your chest.

5. Rub your hands together, up and down, vigorously to generate heat, and then separate your hands from one another, keeping them at heart-level and about six inches apart, as if holding a ball or a block between them. No need to get out a ruler; it's just a guideline. Hand, wrist, and forearm are in a straight line. There's some space under your armpits; elbows are neither too close nor too far away from your body.

6. In your mind's eye, picture that your hands, and your heart, are huge. Hold for at least three minutes if possible, breathing naturally, relaxing and softening your belly, feeling like you have big hands and a big heart.

7. After a few minutes, slightly and very slowly pulse your hands toward and away from each other. Focus on the palms of your hands and notice what you feel.

8. Bring your hands back to stillness for a moment, and then slowly bring them back down to your lap.

Please note: Steps 1–3 are a good foundation for any seated guided practice.

Bonus: You may also visit www.rebeccacliogould.com/bookbonus *for a video demonstration.*

During this practice, my students will often say they feel like there's something between their hands, as if it's hard to bring them closer to one another. Some feel tingling or warmth and a feeling of movement between their hands even when holding still and not pulsing. If you didn't feel anything, don't worry about it. Just keep practicing, and most importantly, keep an open mind. Whether you feel it or not, it's there.

Qi is all around you and inside of you. This is not magic or some made-up concept for people to either believe in or not. Qi is real. It's challenging to measure or test it scientifically, but EKG and MRI do measure the electromagnetic field of the heart and brain. Plus, the proven health benefits of acupuncture, tai chi, and qigong help verify the existence of this vital life-force energy and the healing powers that come from working with it.

And, congratulations, if you did feel it! The "force" is now with you. The truth is it's always with you. But now it's time to use it more consciously, and the palpable experience of qi, while it isn't required, will assist with consciously utilizing this life-force energy. Cultivating and harnessing it will allow you to feel fueled up and filled up without stuffing yourself with excess calories or caffeine. It can also bring more intensity to the pleasure of lovemaking, self-pleasuring, or simply delighting in a gentle breeze.

Types of Energy

Qi is a sort of umbrella term for energy; however, there are various types that interact with one another. The one of primary interest for us here is *jing*, which world-renowned teacher and author Mantak Chia defines as "sexual, creative, generative energy." Throughout this book, I'll mostly be using the terms "sexual energy" and "orgasmic energy" rather than "jing." Some say that sexual energy and qi *are* the same thing, and that there's no need to distinguish between them. However, according to Chia, there's a bit more to it than that: sexual energy is *jing* and "is converted into [more] life-force energy for the organs, which is called [qi]." An abundance of jing also helps strengthen and calm the spirit or the mind (*shen*, which is another type of qi). And since qi transforms food to feed jing, what we eat absolutely affects our sexual energy.

Why does this matter? Because there is an acknowledgment here of the power and importance of sexual energy as well as a connection between diet and sexuality. Just as the sex act itself is what creates life, *sexual* energy is what creates more vital life-force energy within one's body. This highlights how crucial it is to be conscious of, and intentional with, your sexuality, which is vital to your health and well-being and to your overall energy level and sense of vitality.

Getting in touch with these energies will help you have the energy to live life to the fullest and be your healthiest, happiest, sexiest you. It's not a quick fix or a one-time thing, though; learning to cultivate qi on a *daily basis* is what will yield optimal results. There are various practices provided here for building up your awareness of qi and fortifying your energy reserves so that you'll be both wanting and able to engage more fully with life.

As for *orgasmic energy* or *sexual energy* specifically, think about how it feels to be around someone you're attracted to, someone you sexually crave. Do you feel some heat in your chest, a quickening heart rate, a tingling or pulsation in your yoni, a spark of life flowing through you? Although it may be hard to articulate this type of energy, you can certainly feel or imagine it. And it doesn't necessarily require being around someone who turns you on. This book will help you tap into this energy regardless of what you're doing, where you are, or who you're with. For example, I feel this energy when all alone walking through the woods!

The truth is, sexual energy does not necessarily involve what we tend to think of as *sexual* arousal. It's so much more than that. That being said, my favorite way to describe sexual energy, for the purposes of this book, is as a feeling of titillation and excitement, delight, creative impulse, expansiveness, and even as a driving force that propels you into action. Orgasmic energy, while similar to sexual energy in many ways, is what I refer to as the feeling of passion, exhilaration, and pleasure when your qi is flowing and your senses are awakened and "turned on." The physical sensation of this energy may be mostly in your genitals and other erogenous zones, but with conscious awareness, you'll be able to feel this throughout your entire body; you will even be able to direct it and help it flow through and out of you in the most beneficial of ways, to feel good throughout the day and create the life of pleasure and joy you desire.

Another type of energy you'll learn to cultivate is *love energy*. Specifically, the energy of unconditional love. According to Master Li Junfeng, founder of the International Sheng Zhen Society (pronounced "shung jen"), love is the most basic and original energy of the Universe. From love came qi. And from love and qi came life. This love energy is crucial to your overall sense of health and well-being, and we will explore it more throughout this book.

Quality of Energy

Since one of the primary sources of qi is found in the food we eat, it is important to consider food quality and quantity. Being mindful of the energy you take in through your food is one way to cultivate higher quality qi. And it's important to consider how you take care of yourself and "use" yourself throughout the day when it comes to all of your actions (and your inactions, too).

One popular analogy is that of a car. Consider the different types and brands of gasoline and how to get the most mileage. It depends on how you drive as well as the type of gasoline you buy and the kind of maintenance the car receives. Thus, in addition to looking at the quality of food and anything else you put into your body, you also need to consider how you use and treat your body.

Do you fill yourself with empty calories by eating processed foods full of refined flours and sweeteners? Or do you eat whole foods that are rich in nutrients? Do you run yourself ragged or take time to relax and enjoy life? Do you think loving thoughts toward yourself? Do you get enough movement throughout the day? These things matter because *everything* you do, even what you *think*, affects your energy, which in turn affects your health, happiness, and overall sense of sexiness and well-being.

I'll give you an example of how this plays out with eating: if I crave ice cream and buy a pint of Ben & Jerry's, I can devour it all and then feel crappy afterward because it's full of sugar and isn't the highest quality "fuel" for my system. But if I buy a pint of Coconut Bliss (non-dairy ice cream made from coconut milk and sweetened with agave) because it's actually a healthier, more nutritious option, I can barely even eat a suggested serving of it. Instead, I feel satisfied after a couple of spoons-full rather than a couple of bowls-full because it's so rich—the texture, the sweetness, and the heaviness from the coconut milk make my body (and tongue) feel just right. And it doesn't deplete me or leave me feeling bad physically or emotionally. So if ice cream is a weakness of yours, I suggest you try this type of substitution the next time you have a craving. It works! And look for more on cravings in chapter 9.

Qigong and Energy Cultivation

There are many ways to build up and enhance the quality of your energy. Simply being aware and intentional with your food choices is one way. Another? Qigong, pronounced "chee gung."

Qigong is an ancient system of qi cultivation that uses movement, breath, and the power of the mind to exchange qi with the Universe. Qigong is good for overall health and well-being as it's an interchange of dis-eased qi for fresh, pure, healthy universal qi. There are many systems of qigong, but the primary system I practice and teach is Sheng Zhen Gong (sounds like "shung jen gung"), the Qigong of Unconditional Love. Sheng Zhen opens the heart and elevates one's spirit. It removes negativities that lead to worry, sadness, anger, nervousness, fear, and a stressful life by cleaning the qi, purifying and strengthening the mind, and removing blockages by getting the qi flowing.

In chapter 5, you will learn more about Sheng Zhen because this will be one of the foundational practices for the Multi-Orgasmic Diet. Why? Because Sheng Zhen Gong cleans your energy and reduces stress by helping you relax your body and mind, open your heart, and let go of whatever is weighing you down or holding you back. Sheng Zhen teaches you to tap into your sweet, soulful bliss and feel more love and enjoyment—all of which will help you feel sexier and lead to you making healthier choices, as a bonus to the three primary functions and purposes of Sheng Zhen, which are to heal the body, balance the emotions, and elevate one's spirit.

You will learn more about Sheng Zhen later, but for now, try the simple movement of the Gathering Qi practice to bring more qi into your body.

Practice:

GATHERING QI

The Gathering Qi practice can be found in various systems of qigong. When done in Sheng Zhen, the movements (like all Sheng Zhen movements) are also done with love. Sheng Zhen Gong has nine steps, and the first step includes Gathering Qi. The following is a simplified version of this movement for beginners.

1. Stand or sit comfortably with your feet flat on the floor, spine straight. Allow your arms to hang down at your sides. Turn your palms upward and spread your fingers apart. Stretch your arms out to the sides as you take a long and deep inhalation. Keep your chin slightly lifted.

2. While inhaling, continue moving the arms upward and gradually arc your arms inward until your hands are above your head, palms facing down toward the top of the head. Middle fingertips should point toward each other but not touch.

3. While exhaling, bring your hands closer to each other (still not touching) as they continue to move down, palms facing down, in front of the body.

4. As your hands come down toward your lower belly, part them to the sides and turn your palms to face up as your hands continue to move upward again.

Repeat several times, and then simply relax for a few moments. Sit down or lean back, and just allow the qi to circulate, noticing how you feel.

Note: When gathering qi, really feel or imagine that you are bringing healing energy from the Universe into your body. This practice may be done seated or standing. Do your best to let go of thoughts and worries and simply enjoy practicing these mindful movements.

Visit www.rebeccacliogould.com/bookbonus for a demo of this simplified version. Or, for the full practice of Gathering Qi, visit www.shengzhen.org.

In addition to bringing more qi into your body, Gathering Qi is a simple yet profound technique for grounding, centering, and both energizing and relaxing yourself. For optimal benefit, it's important to practice qigong every day, even if just one movement for a few minutes. Just like you eat daily to take in nutrition, and use the bathroom daily to eliminate waste, bringing in fresh, pure, healing qi and sending out stagnant, murky qi will help you feel your best. And Gathering Qi is a super easy practice to do on a daily basis. As few as three slow and intentional repetitions will make a difference.

The Bouncy Shake practice is also a quick and easy way to get more in touch with qi any time as you go through your day.

Practice:

BOUNCY SHAKE

Stand with your feet hip distance apart or a little wider. Let your knees be soft, not locked straight. Bounce up and down, with feet planted flat on the ground. Shaking up and down like this helps get the qi flowing.

While shaking, you may notice areas of stiffness. Just notice them. No judgment. Shake as gently or vigorously as you like. You also might start coughing or passing gas; let it happen. As qi circulates in the body, it gets things moving, and that can lead to burps, farts, coughs, etcetera.

After shaking for three to five minutes, or longer, stop. Stand still. Notice what you feel.

Option: Since one source of qi is the planet Earth itself, intentionally connecting to the Earth and drawing Earth energy up into your body is one way to harness this powerful living source. Think about how Earth sustains so many life forms. Bring this energy up through your feet and through your entire body. Some people like to visualize qi as light or a color or combination of colors; see this qi traveling through you, filling you up, energizing, nurturing, and satisfying you.

This practice is also known as bio-energetic shaking. It's found in various systems of qigong and can be used on its own. I first learned an exercise similar to this called "Shake It" from Jeff Primack, founder of Supreme Science Qigong. In addition to shaking being an exercise used in various qigong systems, it is also taught in Shakti Malan's "Awakening Your Feminine Sexual Essence" course as a way to connect to the Earth element. This Earth connection makes you feel more supported, which helps you relax and open up to your flow of sexual energy. And when you develop your capacity to feel your sexual energy flowing through you, you'll feel more titillated all throughout your day!

So this week, start adding Bouncy Shake and Gathering Qi to your daily routine, prior to meals, or when unhealthy cravings arise. My students and clients report feeling more grounded, focused, and calm while also feeling more energized when implementing these exercises. Now is also a great time to start creating a menu. You can jump ahead to chapter 12 or access a menu template in your book bonuses.

Sacred Energy Exchange

Pretty much everything in life consists of an energy exchange. Eating. Your relationships. Even money. The money you pay for goods and services is an energy exchange. Sex is an energy exchange. Conversation is an energy exchange. Qigong is an energy exchange. You get the point?

But what's so *sacred* about it? No matter what your religious or spiritual beliefs are, let's just say that sacredness is about the consciousness you bring to anything you do. It's also about the level at which you honor yourself and others in all of your activities. Sacred sexuality involves tapping into your full aliveness by embracing, rather than denying, how crucial sexuality is to your well-being and sense of fulfillment.

When you consistently connect with yourself as a sacred being and value this life as a precious gift, the choices you make will be more aligned with what serves your highest purpose. Sometimes that will be to indulge in a pint of ice cream. But more often than not, it will instead be to choose healthy, whole foods that satisfy you and fill you with fresh, pure, vital life-force energy, helping you feel more vibrantly alive.

As you raise your awareness and consciousness, you will, as a byproduct, start putting healthier foods into your body. You might also find that your relationships change when getting clear about the energy exchange taking place. If any of your relationships are draining, toxic, one-sided, or otherwise unhealthy, you'll find yourself needing to distance yourself or sever ties. These relationships simply will no longer resonate, or the already present dissonance will increase to a point of no longer being tolerable. Sometimes you don't even need to take action; sometimes the other person will suddenly leave or gradually fade away without you needing to say or do anything. Although it can feel challenging when relationships end or change, and although there may be some resistance and grief, you will notice an overall improvement in how you feel once the dust settles. There will be more time and space and energy freed up for you to experience and delight in the multi-orgasmic potential of life.

Sacred energy exchange is also, of course, about S E X. Sacred Energy eXchange. Get it? When we connect with another person sexually, the exchange of energy is amplified and can be far more intimate than in other forms of interaction. Even when there is no physical penetration, there is a transmission of energy in which you are the receiver. Therefore, it's important to consider the energy of your partner. And by getting familiar with your own sexual energy, improving its quality, and learning to harness it, your sexual encounters will improve.

By viewing this all as sacred—whether you delight in one-night stands or in celibacy—the cultural conditioning of shame and taboo will also fall away more easily. Keep remembering that sexual power and pleasure are your birthright. Sex brought you into the world. You are a sexual being, and that is a beautiful, wonderful thing.

Another consideration is that women typically get energized from sex, and men get depleted. However, if a man learns Tantric sexual practices or Taoist sexual arts, although there is a transfer of energy, he's less likely to feel depleted or tired after sex. Books like *The Multi-Orgasmic Man* and *The Tao of Health, Sex, and Longevity* are great resources for the men in your life as well as for women in same-sex partnerships who exert more masculine energy.

For now, just start noticing how you feel after sex with a partner or with yourself. Do you feel energized with one, but not the other?

Do you feel energized after both (or neither)? I want you to start raising your awareness little by little as you play with the concepts and practices presented in these pages. When you're ready to go deeper—if you want to go deeper—into sexual cultivation practices specifically, *Sexual Awakening for Women, The Multi-Orgasmic Woman,* or *Healing Love Through the Tao* are all good options. And *The Multi-Orgasmic Diet* is a great place to start preparing yourself for the more advanced concepts and techniques you'll find in those books. I also recommend reading the article "Why is Sex Sacred," by Dr. Deborah Taj Anapol; it's included in the Resources.

Revisiting the Link Between Sexual Energy and Anxiety

Whether you tend toward anxiety or not, it's useful to look at the link between sexual energy and anxiety. There are all sorts of reasons people feel anxiety, whether it's high- or low-level. But the one common source people may not even realize? The blockage of sexual energy.

As Wilhelm Reich explains in *The Function of the Orgasm,* when the flow of sexual energy is hindered, neuroses develop. You don't need to be certifiably neurotic, clinically depressed, or have an anxiety disorder to apply this to yourself. The point Reich makes is that your mental, emotional, and physical well-being are directly affected by whether or not your sexual energy is flowing and being expressed freely in healthy ways.

What does this have to do with anything? What does this have to do with diet, lifestyle, and living life to the fullest? One sign of sexual energy blockage is obvious or low-level anxiety or depression that contributes to making unhealthy choices, such as self-medicating with food. Sexual energy may be blocked through conscious suppression, unconscious repression, or cultural oppression. It can also be obstructed when one's attempts at love, sexual gratification, and sexual expression are thwarted by others or by the lack of another. When this sexual energy is blocked, its ability to generate more qi for your organs is compromised; your sense of vitality, creativity, and excitement is not going to be at its fullest capacity.

We are sexual beings, sexual creatures, here to experience love, connection, and pleasure. And when this essential part of who you are, of your magnificence, is hindered or kept small for any reason, you are not living up to your fullest potential. It doesn't mean that you need to be having sex or masturbating or having peak orgasms on a regular basis. But it does mean that it's important to be in touch with this core part of yourself and to develop a healthy relationship with your sexuality. It's important to cultivate healthy outlets and ways of expressing your sexual energy, sexual urges, and your very basic and human needs for love and sexual gratification.

Reich goes so far as to say that your potency in any and all areas of life can be directly related to your sexual potency. I'd extend that to say that if you want to live life to your fullest potential, but something's been stopping you, it very well may be a sexual energy blockage, in which case it's time for some sexual healing. Although sometimes there's far more to the picture than what this book covers, such as a need for nutritional supplementation or psychotherapy, for you this book may be all it takes. For you, relieving anxiety and healing sexually *may* be as simple as getting more in touch with your body, cultivating qi, awakening the senses, and learning to deeply and truly relax and fall in love with yourself and with all of life.

Learning to Relax

Relaxation is crucial to energy flow as well as to pleasure. When you're tight and tense, energy doesn't flow as well, and it's hard to actually feel your feelings emotionally or physically. Imagine water running through a hose. Now imagine something has fallen on that hose, or there's a kink in it which either fully blocks the flow or leaves just a little bit of space for the water to keep moving through. This happens inside of you, too, in terms of your sexual energy and qi. There are many relaxation techniques out there, and qigong also focuses on getting you to relax your body. I invite you now to take a few minutes to try this practice of softening your body and feeling or visualizing the energy flowing inside you.

Practice:

FULL-BODY RELAXATION & ENERGY FLOW

Part 1: Lie down and close your eyes. Progressively relax your body from head to toe. Start by feeling the crown of your head softening and continue down your entire body. Feel or imagine any knots of tension getting smaller with each breath and dissolving away. Let any tension in your body melt away like candle wax dripping down a candle. Feel your whole body fully relax, feeling heavy, soft, and loose.

Part 2: Bring your attention to the centers of the soles of your feet. Picture a little window or door opening in them. Picture qi, in the form of light, coming in through your feet and traveling up your legs through your yoni and pelvis and into your lower belly, into the dantian.*

Picture the dantian as about the size of a tennis ball. And for this practice, picture it as a ball of light.

Continue allowing this qi to travel in through your feet to the dantian as you bring your attention to the centers of the palms of your hands. Open the windows or doors there, and see qi traveling in through your palms, up your arms, down through your heart, and into your lower belly, into the dantian.

As the qi continues traveling in through your feet and your palms, bring your attention to the crown of your head. Feel or imagine the crown of your head opening, bringing in more qi, and see that qi travel down through your head and your neck, passing through your heart, and entering the dantian.

Continue softening and relaxing your body as you feel or visualize this energy flowing through you. Over time, the more you soften and relax and can truly feel the qi, the more pleasure you will find in this practice; it may even sexually arouse you.

* The dantian is a storehouse of qi located below and behind the navel. And recall that yoni is the Sanskrit term for vulva, vagina, and womb, and regarded as a symbol of divine procreative power, a symbol of Shakti, the female principle of divine energy.

Visit www.rebeccacliogould.com/bookbonus for the audio-recording of a more detailed version of this practice.

As your sensitivity to feeling the qi increases, this practice will help you detect energy blockages throughout your body and open up to feeling pleasurable currents of vital life-force energy and sexual energy flowing through you. You also might notice that the quality of, or ability to feel, this energy flow is affected by what or how much you eat. If you'd like to run a little experiment, do this practice before and after a meal, or after a healthy meal or snack and then after an unhealthy one. Observe how you feel after each.

Harnessing Energy and Outlets for Sexual Energy

As you become more conscious of this energy inside and around you, you will feel more powerful. Harnessing energy regards producing, controlling, and making use of qi and sexual energy. Learning to harness your energy will help you live a more fulfilling life. Simply bringing more awareness—questioning how you are expending or directing your energy—can have a big impact, too.

When you get in touch with your own energy—specifically your sex energy, your orgasmic energy—you'll be amazed by how much more confident, happy, and powerful you feel. It might even be scary at first. *What to do with this energy?* Anything and everything you want, dear. That's what. But I'll also provide some guidance and suggestions in the following chapters, and below. So keep going.

It's essential to your health and overall well-being that your sexual energy flows freely, and that you have healthy outlets and ways to experience a sense of gratification whether partnered or single, sexually active or not. Perhaps you don't have a sexual partner, or you feel that your needs aren't being met even if you do. And perhaps masturbation or orgasm are not always an option for you. Or maybe you're just not in the mood, and that's okay. Have no fear!

Sexual energy doesn't need to be expressed through the sex act itself. It can be expressed through acts of creation or through physical activity. It can even be expressed simply by consciously allowing the energy to flow through you, by letting yourself feel it and be fueled and delighted by it, such as in the Full-Body Relaxation exercise discussed earlier, or in the Sex Energy Circulation practice here.

Practice:

SEX ENERGY CIRCULATION

The next time you feel aroused by something, whether by a person, a song, a brownie, or a massage, try this to become more aware of the sexual energy being stirred up and to learn how to circulate it:

1. Take a deep breath. Shut your eyes if possible. If not, keep them open. Continue breathing deeply. Breathe your arousal in, and breathe into your arousal. Breathe down into your nipples. Breathe down into your yoni.

2. Picture this sexual energy, this arousal, like light flowing through you. Focus in on where you feel it in your body. Do you feel it primarily in your breasts? In your yoni? In your mind? In your eyes? In your throat? In your mouth? Somewhere else?

3. Wherever it is, focus on it. And if it's all throughout your body or in multiple places, that's fine. But for now, just focus on one location.

4. From that location, you have two options (you may even start with the first one and then continue with the second):

    a. With each breath, see that energy flowing from that one location to all other parts of your body, traveling from organ to organ, bone to bone, body part to body part, lighting up each and every part of you; or

    b. On the inhale, see the light in that one spot getting brighter, and on the exhale, see the light expanding. Continue breathing and visualizing in this way until you are full of this energy, full of light.

5. When you feel complete with step 4, notice how you feel. Do you feel more energized, satisfied, or inspired?

The conscious awareness of this energy flow can happen along with any sort of daily activity, not just in a guided practice. It can also arise organically as part of your meditation, qigong, or breathwork experience; as you raise your awareness and become more sensitive to your own energy flow, you may notice feelings of sexual arousal during "nonsexual" activities. Let yourself feel it. Let it flow instead of trying to stop it or deny it.

What matters most is not the way in which you get this energy flowing, but simply that you *do* get it moving and find ways to delight in it—to delight in life, experience more pleasure, and feel more comfortable and free in expressing your sexuality. If you have pent-up sexual energy, it can manifest as anxiety, depression, irritability, and insomnia, all of which can lead to emotional eating. Needless to say, it's important to do something with this energy and get it flowing, regardless of how and regardless of your relationship status or ability to orgasm.

The main outlets I suggest are:

1. **Sex/Masturbation:** Obviously, you may not always be able to have sex when you want it—unless you have a sex slave, in which case more power to you. But it does take two to tango. So if there isn't a partner, or if that partner isn't available, or if that partner just isn't "doing it" for you, you can always take matters into your own hands. Pun intended.

   More on masturbation in chapter 8. For now, I'll just encourage you to touch yourself whenever the mood arises. Whenever you feel turned on, do something about it. The other option is to breathe through it, feeling the energy flowing and circulating that sex energy through you, channeling it for use in other ways. But *do* play around with playing with yourself when you can.

2. **Movement:** Movement is one of the best ways to move energy. Even if you're not having sex or masturbating, you can move your body as if you are, such as by spiraling your spine, undulating your hips, and rocking your pelvis. You can also shake, as a practice. Or do some cardio. Go for a hike. Do some jumping jacks. Or dance it out. More on this in chapter 10. Qigong is also a form of movement that is specifically designed to get the qi unblocked and flowing, and although there are many systems of qigong out there, I highly recommend Sheng Zhen because of its focus on opening the heart.

3. **Breath, with or without Vocalization:** Breath is an essential part of cultivating and harnessing your sexual energy and feeling more pleasure. Conscious breath can also short-circuit cravings, calm the mind, and help you eat more slowly. Exhaling with sound and making sounds is one of the best ways to move energy that's stuck in your body in the form of negative emotions. It could be as simple as a loud sigh or as edge-pushing as a lioness roar. We'll explore breath and using your voice in various chapters.

4. **Creation:** As a woman, you are meant to create. And you don't need to create a baby. You just need to create. Feeling like you have pent-up energy? Breathe into it and pour it into a creative endeavor. Creation is one of the best ways to prevent over-consumption, or in other words, to prevent overeating or binge eating. Sometimes when energy is pent up, especially sexual energy, we turn toward sweets or other foods that aren't so good for us. Why? Not only because it's comforting, but also because it numbs us out and further suppresses that energy, which in the moment feels good but in the long run is not an effective coping strategy. More on this in chapter 9.

These are also all good things to do when cravings arise, before giving in to snacking, or before a meal. For now, this is just some food for thought before diving deeper in the coming pages.

ANY AND ALL OF the practices in this chapter can be part of your Multi-Orgasmic Diet plan. Start practicing some of them before meals or snacks, when cravings arise, or when you feel like you need an energy boost, and see what happens.

You can do the Bouncy Shake or Gathering Qi practice prior to each meal or snack as well as when you feel a strong desire to eat something unhealthy. You can also use these practices if feeling low in energy, anxious, or down in the dumps.

Pay attention to how this affects the way you feel and what, or how much, you eat. And continue working on time management and slowing down.

Visit www.rebeccacliogould.com/bookbonus for the practice contract template as well as a sample menu plan that includes the practices shared up to this point. And know that you are well on your way to living a multi-orgasmic life!

Chapter 3

ORGASM ~ THE PULSE AND PLEASURE OF LIFE

"The pleasure of living and the pleasure of orgasm are identical."

~ WILHELM REICH

Time to talk about the Big O, starting with an invitation to think outside the box and open up to new ways of defining and experiencing orgasm. And if you don't easily orgasm or have never experienced it at all or in the way you'd like to, don't worry. Just keep reading with an open mind and keep breathing. Although I won't be teaching you explicitly how to "achieve orgasm" in the traditional sense, in the next chapter, and throughout the book, you will learn how to handle barriers to orgasm and orgasmic energy. I will also share techniques that you can use to enhance your pleasure potential and your ability to live a multi-orgasmic life both in and out of the bedroom.

Remember that multi-orgasmic *living* is about living a life full of heightened awareness and pleasure, a life in which you feel energized and in touch with yourself and have an attitude of saying "yes, oh yes!" whenever possible. And multi-orgasmic dieting is about getting into a routine of practices designed to give you a multi-orgasmic life so that you feel energized and fulfilled throughout your day, which means less overeating or compulsive eating to self-soothe, self-sabotage, or fill a void.

All of that being said, if you're orgasmic in the traditional sense of the word and ready to play around with layering genital-centered orgasm into your diet plan, go for it. If you've already started creating your own menu plan, you can add in "masturbation" before snacks or as a substitution for them. You might also start your day with it as part of a morning routine or masturbate anytime throughout the day to see how it affects your mood and energy level, as well as your meal and snack choices, which can actually be triggered by a deep, intrinsic need for pleasure. More on that later, though; right now, it's time to clarify some terms.

Common Definitions and Cultural Conditioning

Perhaps the preceding pages have already got you thinking differently, but what images or feelings flow through you in response to the word "orgasm"? Toe-curling, spine-tingling, skin-against-skin quakes of pleasure? Softness, hardness, dryness, wetness, sliding, undulating, thrusting, sucking, licking, and a big release at the end?

The Merriam-Webster dictionary defines orgasm as the way in which you're probably used to thinking of it: "a climax of sexual excitement, characterized by feelings of pleasure centered in the genitals and (in men) experienced as an accompaniment to ejaculation." However, I want you to consider orgasm as going beyond the genitals, and sometimes having nothing to do, at least not directly or obviously, with them. And that's why I prefer Dictionary.com's definition, as it also includes the possibility of defining orgasm as "intense or unrestrained excitement," period, plain and simple.

Furthermore, even if orgasm is defined as the climax or peak of sexual excitation, who's to say what that looks or feels like? Who's to say you need to cum and have that full-release type of experience? Sometimes it's actually better *not* to have that grand finale and instead circulate that energy and channel it into other endeavors.

Or what if the peak of your sexual excitation is a smile or a surge of energy or laughter, a revelation or insight, or even a blissfully calm feeling? All of these can be experienced in a variety of situations or places—and none of them necessarily need to be perceived as sexual.

While it's beneficial to work on—and play with—practices for enhancing genital-centered orgasms, and I encourage you to do so, *The Multi-Orgasmic Diet* focuses on tapping into your sexual energy in order to experience more intense and unrestrained excitement and pleasure in all areas of your life. I want you to stimulate more than just your genitals or primary erogenous zones. I want your life to feel more *orgasmic*, and that can be defined simply as "very enjoyable or exciting."

As for *multi*-orgasmic, what does that conjure up for you? Is it something you experience? Does the thought of it excite or intrigue you, or does it sound elusive and unobtainable? Interestingly, multi-orgasmic is in the medical dictionary section of Merriam-Webster, and on collinsdictionary.com, the definition is "having or able to have more than one orgasm during sexual intercourse." The accompanying sentence example even gives a statistic for the number of people who are believed to be multi-orgasmic. By the way, it's "15 to 25 percent of the population." However, if we redefine this word to simply mean the capacity to experience multiple instances of enjoyment and excitation—whether or not during sex—then the multi-orgasmic population grows by leaps and bounds.

And you absolutely have the right to shift your thinking about what's orgasmic. Words have power, and how you define them and embody their meanings just might create dramatic changes in your life. When you consider the words "intense or unrestrained excitement" or "enjoyment and excitation," what does that look like for you? I encourage you to define some terms for yourself.

Practice:

DEFINING YOUR OWN TERMS

Think about or write out answers to these questions:

1. How have you defined orgasm in the past? How do you experience it?

2. How would you like to define and experience orgasm for yourself now?

3. What have you always thought of as *multi-orgasmic,* and how would you like to define it now?

4. What do you consider *sexy*?

5. What does *pleasure* feel like to you?

These questions are meant to help you open your mind as well as your body to more ways of experiencing ecstasy and feeling satisfied by the pulses of life flowing through you. Don't worry if you don't have clear answers right away; you can always come back to this later or let these questions remain as open curiosities as you live your life.

Definition for This Book

If you're a fan of yoga, meditation, or any other mindfulness practices, you probably know that some of the objectives include getting in touch with what you feel in your body and what you desire, as well as cultivating a deeper sense of connection and pleasure with all aspects of life. For now, when you think of orgasm, consider those objectives but remove the requirement to climax—where you rise up to a huge peak, explode, and then crash afterward. Instead, view each moment as an opportunity to have an orgasmic experience.

When I started writing this book, I knew I wanted to share my expanded view of orgasm with other women since so many of us narrowly define it in that peak/explosion manner. I view orgasm as something that can be about more than sex and masturbation; it does not need to be a solely genital-induced experience. Orgasm is about energy flow and pleasure. Orgasmic energy is "exciting and enjoyable" energy flowing through you, and it can come simply from letting life stimulate and arouse you. Orgasm is the pulse of life.

Imagine waking up in the morning, luxuriating in the feel of the sheets against your skin, delighting in how it feels to be held by your bed, and noticing a smile starting to form on your face. Maybe you even caress yourself a little or go all out into some morning masturbation or lovemaking. And then you catch your reflection in the mirror, smile at your own beauty, blush, and notice a little tingle flowing through you, and some heat, too, as you turn yourself on. In these moments, you breathe in and feel more fully alive—and sexy! And it doesn't stop there. As you go throughout your day, even the little things will fill you up with pleasure and joy.

This is just one example of what it's like to be multi-orgasmic. It's about your ability to **feel and surrender to the ecstasy of energy flow, expression, and release** all throughout the day, all throughout your life. It's about experiencing various instances of unrestrained, intense excitement and joy thanks to cultivating and harnessing your sexual energy and awakening your senses.

Being multi-orgasmic means you're open and receptive to being delighted and turned on, and the Multi-Orgasmic *Diet* is about having numerous times a day where you consciously experience arousal and pleasure—whether it's before, during, or after eating but ideally some combination of the three—as a way to develop healthier eating habits and enjoyment of food. By connecting with your sexual energy, and feeling orgasmic energy flowing through you prior to eating a meal or a snack, you're more likely to make healthier food choices—including when and how much to eat—and to enjoy the act of eating more while feeling happy, satisfied, and fulfilled.

Riding the Energy of Your Valleys and Peaks

While it's typical to contract into the type of full-release orgasm most women are accustomed to, known as a *peak* orgasm, being multi-orgasmic doesn't necessarily mean doing *that* multiple times. Lingering in the valleys along the way and allowing the energy to flow, build, ebb, and flow and flow and build and release—through contractions, relaxation, and dissipation or circulation of energy—is all part of being multi-orgasmic.

The standard peak orgasms, that result in climax, tend to be brought on by contraction, a tightening up to force that intense, explosive type of orgasm. And that's fine. But also try relaxing and riding out the waves. Play around with focusing on the pleasure of getting there, on the journey rather than the destination. This will help you relax and experience more joy in sex, masturbation, and all of life. Enjoy the ride. I'm inviting you to hang out in the valleys on and off throughout your day, wherever you are, whatever you're doing.

Exploring the Yearning to Be Unrestrained

There's a word above that I want to highlight: unrestrained. Typically, what's so euphoric and intense about orgasm is that it just might be one of the only times, if not *the* only time, you fully let go in life. Many women hold back sexually, especially when it comes to orgasm, but also just in the way they exude, or rather inhibit, their sexual energy and feminine sensuality. Part of what's going on here is that you have this energy inside of you called *Shakti*—a feminine energy—and one of its key traits is that it cannot be contained. And yet so many women in our society *do* contain their Shakti, their feminine sexual vibrancy and powerful creative force. This leads to all kinds of dissatisfaction in life.

And self-consciousness is one of the biggies when it comes to reasons women hold back. So getting over that feeling is a crucial part of living life to the fullest and becoming sexually free. My teacher Shakti Malan talks about an image of the "unleashed feminine" writhing around on the floor. And why shouldn't we get into our animal bodies, let go of inhibitions, and writhe around with abandon? We'll ponder this more in chapter 4, but for now, just imagine it's totally safe and natural to do so. Imagine feeling unrestrained and intensely excited all throughout your day, all throughout your life. What if, like a little kid getting an ice cream cone or seeing a puppy, you could feel giddy and excited, full of energy, without holding back? What if the sight of beautiful flowers or the warmth of the sun on your skin resulted in feeling your sexual energy running through you, enlivening you, whether it leads you to the bedroom or not? This is possible, and you may even learn to feel this without anything other than the stimulation of your own breath or conscious awareness.

While most diet books would encourage restraint, I say screw that. What I've seen in myself and in clients is that when living a life full of pleasure, joy, and fun, there is less need to fill a void with, numb out with, or artificially energize with food. So don't hold back.

Now, let's explore what it means to be unrestrained, unleashed, uncontained.

Practice:

UNRESTRAINED

Because the main part of this practice may feel a bit edgy so soon in this journey, I'm giving you a journaling practice before asking you to drop deeply into your body and let your Shakti flow:

1. First, make a list of areas in your life or the ways in which you hold back.

2. Next, write about how things would look and what you'd feel like if you didn't hold back.

3. Reflect on the previous two steps. What concerns and fears arise? What excitement and elation arises?

And now? Let go.

Put on some sexy music and dance around wildly, seductively. Feel the music moving through you; let the music move you. Or get on the floor and actually writhe around!

Other options are to walk around your house naked, or sing a song at the top of your lungs even if it's off key. Or do some combination of these things! The point is to let loose and feel the exhilaration of doing so.

Opening Up to Pleasure and Saying Yes to Life

How capable are you of surrendering and experiencing pleasure? Seems pretty straightforward, but you might not realize that surrendering is essential for your health, energy flow, and ability to feel bliss. This has a lot to do with how orgasmic you are (or aren't), or as Reich puts it, your "orgastic potency." Opening up to pleasure means opening up to life's delights and the energy they contain. When you deny pleasure, you deny life. And vice versa. If you're shutting down or keeping pleasure at bay, you're essentially saying that you don't really want to live.

Simply sitting in recognition of what a gift it is to be alive, and feeling life-force energy flowing through your body, can be orgasmic and can fill you with ecstatic bliss.

Practice:

SAYING YES TO LIFE

Practice saying the word "yes" more and more, especially saying it out loud, "Yes! Oh, yes! God, yes!" Have fun with it. Entertain yourself with it. Make yourself laugh. This will raise your vibration, bringing you more fully into alignment with the Yes-ness of life and your pleasure potential.

If you're experiencing any repression or frigidity, saying yes to life and opening yourself to the pleasure all around you can also help with actual clitoral or vaginal orgasm. Experiment with feeling and expressing delight, and even be witnessed in it. Let others see and hear you express how good you feel. This might sound scary or "wrong" if you think there are only certain places or situations in which it's okay to be sexually aroused. But while you may need to control yourself in certain contexts, at least to some extent, you can still allow yourself to have your own inner, personal pleasure experience rather than shutting it down completely. Let it fill you up as life-force energy. Let it energize you and uplift you. Let it make you glow even if you have to suppress a moan to remain "professional" or "respectful."

Practice:

VOCALIZING PLEASURE

Vocal expression and sexual pleasure are directly related. Vocalizing your pleasure helps reinforce what you're experiencing—and that's good for both you and your lover.

Begin in private. Moan in delight when you eat something yummy, smell a fragrance you like, or climb into bed ('cuz it feels so good to lie down). You can start off with just a short "Mm" or "Yum." Then try it when sharing a meal with someone. Or when smelling someone during an embrace. Or getting into bed with someone. Moan in delight and/or say, "Oh that feels/smells/tastes sooooo good." Before you know it, you'll find it easier and easier to vocalize pleasure and even ask for what you want.

Another way to say yes to life and receive pleasure is to treat yourself to a professional massage *and* to vocalize your pleasure and satisfaction during it. If you're like me, you may feel too relaxed during a massage to want to open your mouth or let any sounds come out, but this is still a worthy exercise, especially if you feel embarrassed. It's time to gently push your comfort zone as part of your multi-orgasmic life! Plus, getting a massage helps meet your touch needs; when you aren't receiving enough touch, you're more likely to reach for unhealthy food, drinks, or even people, to fill that void.

Practice:

MASSAGE BLISS

Do you allow yourself to experience pleasure while getting a massage, or do you shut down sexually because you want to respect professional boundaries? Never had a massage? Go get one! That's a good way to start opening up to pleasure.

If you feel self-conscious making sounds of pleasure on the table, you can just smile, open up to feeling more, and tell your massage therapist that you're practicing delighting in touch and want to feel free to moan or say "oh, that feels so good" without making him or her uncomfortable.

If getting a professional massage isn't an option for you, or even if it is, I also recommend giving yourself foot massages on a regular basis. You can put this on your menu plan and practice moaning and groaning and oohing and ahhing along with it.

How to Maximize Your Pleasure Potential

One of the best ways to cut down on unhealthy food cravings *and* live a fuller, juicier life is to maximize your pleasure potential. How to do this? Awareness. Intention. Breath. Engaging your senses. And expanding your concept of what you believe, what you even *think of*, as being a pleasure.

Practice:

THE PLEASURE LIST

Step 1. Make a list of *everything* that brings you pleasure—everything that feels good, makes you smile, lights you up, fills you up, satisfies you, tickles you, delights you, excites you. Use a notebook, and write it out by hand. What you write by hand is more connected to your heart, more embodied. Let the words flow out but also take your time with it. Take deep breaths. Get curious. Get creative. This is a first draft, so don't worry how it looks or what order anything is in.

Include activities that involve someone else as well as things that don't. List active and passive options, like going for a walk or thinking about all the things for which you're grateful. And don't forget your indulgences (even those you feel you shouldn't include), like eating an entire pint of ice cream. The point is to see all the things that bring you pleasure, without any judgment or restriction.

Step 2. After you have this rough draft, type it up or rewrite it. Have at least two copies, one to keep on your fridge and one to keep in your purse or in your car. If, for privacy's sake, you don't want to post it, put up a sticky note or a quote magnet that reminds you to look at your list. It could even be a sticky note that says "List."

Refer to your list often to see the abundance of pleasure to be had all throughout your day!

In addition to this list helping you see the many ways to "self-pleasure" and live an orgasmic life, it will also help you find healthier options to quell unhealthy cravings and habits. You'll find more on that later, in chapter 9.

Living a Multi-Orgasmic Life

When we let sexual energy flow freely through us and open ourselves up to feeling *all* of our feelings and sensations, we experience more pleasure—both in and out of the bedroom, both genitally and everywhere else in our bodies, in our cells, in our hearts, minds, and souls.

So I invite you to go beyond the bedroom, beyond that place you think is the only place for sex energy and getting turned on. Feel it everywhere. Even driving in your car. Just imagine the simplest of things giving you a little thrill and qi boost, bringing a smile to your face and more color to your cheeks. Or go beyond imagining it, and experience it:

Practice:

ORGASMIC ORGANS

When you look at something beautiful (like a flower or a sunset), breathe that beauty all the way in and down into your heart, lungs, liver, and so on. Allow it to arouse and enliven you.

Visualize this, perhaps seeing the energy of arousal, your sexual energy, as light. Feel it if you can, perhaps as warmth or a tickle.

When you're delighting in your favorite meal or snack or lover, circulate those pulses of pleasure, sending multiple little love bursts throughout your body and to each organ.

This can be done as a way to curb cravings or prevent yourself from overeating; it's also a good way to fill yourself up with lots of love and sex energy. You just might feel giddy and be glowing after this. It's a great practice to add to your menu.

In terms of orgasm, you can take the above practice further. In *Healing Love Through the Tao*, Mantak Chia writes about each organ having an orgasm in his multi-orgasmic method. Think about it as if sending qi into each organ, and that qi creates an organ orgasm, so to speak. Sending qi to each organ, with the intent of it being like a little burst of pleasure and delight, can be applied to your eating experiences as well as to your sexual experiences.

Additionally, another way to live a multi-orgasmic life is to be aware of, or even plan for, ups and downs, plateaus, momentum, letdowns, releases, relaxation after achievement, and excitement on the buildup of life! The multi-orgasmic life is about riding the waves as well as those climaxes, all the "almost got it, almost there, feels so good, almost there" moments, and then either the letdown of something not happening or the excitement and release when it does. It's not just about awakening your senses and harnessing sex energy but living your life in this dynamic way with lots of peaks and stimulation, ups and downs, and pleasurable momentum building whether you reach those peaks or not—and embracing how alive it all feels and how yummy that is. When you live in this way, filling up on the pleasure of life, you'll feel better about yourself, your body, and what you're eating.

THIS WEEK, START PAYING attention to the ups and downs, the peaks and valleys you experience in your daily life. Also, start opening up to feeling more pleasured and sexually aroused by the simplest of things. Express your delight vocally and step more into that vision of yourself as unrestrained. Delight in all of life!

Chapter 4

OVERCOMING BARRIERS TO ORGASMIC DELIGHT

"The best way out is always through."
~ ROBERT FROST

In the previous chapter, we looked at how orgasm can be seen as a "yes" to pleasure and to life. So can you guess what *difficulty* with orgasm suggests? Yep. Resistance to pleasure and saying "no" to life itself.

Many women have difficulty relaxing, letting go, surrendering, and receiving pleasure, and sometimes there's a medical or dietary reason for that. In fact, in *The Orgasmic Diet*, Marrena Lindberg focuses on dietary and hormonal factors that contribute to orgasm and libido concerns. But if you've already explored those options, or want to start with making *lifestyle* changes, and still feel like your resistance may be something you can overcome on your own, then this chapter may help you learn to surrender and receive more easily.

Remember that although it may occur as a bonus, this book is not about teaching you how to become multi-orgasmic in terms of clitoral or vaginal peak orgasms, but rather about how to feel orgasmic energy and pleasure on and off *all* throughout your day. Ultimately, my hope is that you'll learn to allow yourself to be turned on and aroused by potentially anything, even by the wind or just a good song.

Conditioning and Emotional Armor

It's natural for something that feels good to trigger sexual arousal. However, many of us have been conditioned and shamed out of allowing ourselves to feel delighted by it. We've been taught to suppress and repress, to ignore and deny these feelings. And that dampening down of pleasure can result in trying to fill a void or stimulate ourselves with unhealthy or excessive foods. It can also lead to depression and apathy, which can trigger detrimental eating habits and not being as physically active and energetic as is required for us to be our healthiest, happiest, sexiest selves.

This chapter is dedicated to freeing you from the non-dietary barriers to orgasm, helping you identify underlying roadblocks, and giving you the tools to bust through those blockades. And the practices throughout this entire book will help you open up to experiencing more and more pleasure as you continue on this path because I want you to frequently experience the bubbling up and explosions of delight, excitement, and joy. And remember, orgasm here is not limited to the genitals or to sex. This chapter is about letting go of your resistance to feeling the delight of sexual energy flowing through you—wherever you are, whatever you're doing.

In my experience, both personally and professionally, I see that one's emotional state is one of the biggest barriers to orgasm and to living life to the fullest. This usually appears as some sort of protective mechanism or *emotional armoring*. Armoring also has a physical and energetic component that kicks in to protect you, and yet it actually does more damage and harm by cutting you off from being truly present and able to enjoy the richness and ecstasy of life; it stops you from feeling the flow of living fully alive.

But don't beat yourself up over it. It's nothing to feel bad about; it's a survival mechanism. And you now have the choice to go beyond the reptilian brain and ego-wounding. You have a choice to take off that armor, little by little, as needed and as you're ready to do so.

Inability to Orgasm

There is a variety of misinformation out there regarding women who don't orgasm. In one study I found, researchers said that only ten percent of women have true anorgasmia—the actual *inability* to reach orgasm. The truth is that most women *are* capable of orgasm, but sadly, many women don't. Whether it's because of technique, feeling stressed or pressured or rushed, past sexual trauma, religious or other types of shame, needing more fish oil, having a serotonin/dopamine imbalance, the list goes on and on. And there's help for all of it. As women, we are designed for pleasure, and we all have the potential to orgasm and to be multi-orgasmic. All of us have qi, sexual energy, orgasmic energy flowing through us—well, the flowing part is what comes into question here, but that's something we'll continue to explore.

Numbing Out and Suppressing Sexual Energy Flow

If you're having trouble reaching a peak orgasm or enjoying life to the fullest, you might be numbing out. Perhaps a past trauma is to blame, in which case see the Resources section for more assistance, or perhaps there are other factors. If you're not sure why, that's okay, too; you don't need to know the root cause quite yet. First, simply recognize if there's a lack of feeling—physically, emotionally, or both. And are you eating in a way that numbs you out more, or actually in an attempt to feel something? Suppressing or numbing feelings and energy flow by overeating or eating sweets is a common way of trying to prevent or soothe anxiety. And one of the main culprits for anxiety? Suppression of sexual energy.

As mentioned earlier, when orgasmic energy is blocked, thwarted, or suppressed, anxiety and other neuroses may develop. This sexual energy inside of us is always there, always generating. If we don't let it flow freely through us, tension builds and affects the heart, and that can manifest as a feeling of anxiety. Suppressing arousal stops the energy flow. Therefore, it's crucial to engage in practices that keep the energy flowing so that this stagnation doesn't wreak havoc in your life. We must accept, embrace, and even encourage our sexual feelings and desires.

How to Handle Barriers to Orgasm

First of all, I want to emphasize this: be gentle with yourself. Beating yourself up and feeling not good enough, like there's something wrong with you, or like you're missing out, is not going to help. Thus, the first thing to do is to take the focus off of peak orgasm; let go of agenda. Instead, set yourself up for success by focusing on relaxing and enjoying life while you simply get to know your body and love your body more—and without rushing—through the practices in this book. As we explored in chapter 1, slowing down is key.

You need to feel safe and supported enough to slow down, relax, and open yourself, all of which help to unlock your feminine sexual essence. How to feel safe and supported? To some extent, that's an inside job; you *decide* to feel safe and supported and work on letting go of beliefs that you're not. But there's also an external aspect, such as putting a "do not disturb" sign on your door or turning on loud music or using a white noise machine to give yourself privacy while engaging in some of the practices within this book. And perhaps most important is that you give yourself time and have the patience to change and heal and learn and grow, at your own pace, and as you are ready to do so.

Shame, Guilt, and the Magic of Permission

Shame, which contributes to lack of pleasure and inability to orgasm, is a very low level of consciousness. Dr. David Hawkins, who is known for having mapped and calibrated levels of consciousness, explains this concept at length in *Transcending the Levels of Consciousness*. According to Hawkins, shame is basically the bottom of the barrel, with guilt being just one level higher. Nevertheless, it's important to recognize shame and guilt when we feel them and not let that recognition further shame us. Being ashamed of feeling shame or guilt can be a nasty downward spiral. Instead, in the moment you feel it, give yourself permission.

Marcia Baczynski, sex educator and relationship coach, explains that the intensity will lessen the moment you give yourself permission for a specific thought, feeling, want, action, or desire. It takes the edge off. It gives you space to be with what is. It gives the shame, for example, space to move and dissipate, to be released. And one powerful technique that she shares is the actual creation of *permission slips*. Try it—this works.

Practice:

PERMISSION SLIPS

On an index card or scrap of paper, write the following (or edit as needed):

I hereby grant myself permission to feel shame.
I hereby grant myself permission to NOT feel pleasure.
I hereby grant myself permission to NOT orgasm.

You can then sign it as yourself, as "the Universe," or as someone you want permission from. Or you can ask somebody else to sign it.

You can also experiment with writing another permission slip that is the opposite, such as:

I hereby grant myself permission to NOT feel ashamed.
I hereby grant myself permission to feel pleasure.
I hereby grant myself permission to orgasm.

Feel free to make other permission slips; make as many as you need. They can be permission slips for each practice in this book or just for any practices for which you feel resistant. You can make a permission slip for feeling that resistance as well! I have about a dozen from a workshop with Marcia and still sometimes refer to them over a year later. This permission slip practice has also gotten me in the habit of granting myself permission in the moment, in my head and in my heart, without necessarily needing to reference or create a permission slip. Over time, you will find yourself recognizing when you need permission and giving it to yourself more easily.

Reconnecting with Your Innocence

Because guilt and shame are so heavily programmed into us here in the West and in other parts of the world, you might not even realize they are wreaking havoc. But they probably are. Guilt and shame are like dark entities that can possess you, bring you down, and make you behave in ways that are self-defeating and self-limiting. One way of dealing with them is to get in touch with your innocence and your inner child. That's actually part of why the permission slips are so effective; they speak to that inner child who fears punishment.

However, when you deny yourself the ecstasy and delight of orgasm and of life, *that* is like a punishment. What are you punishing yourself for? How are you treating yourself? Remembering that precious little girl inside just might help the woman in you open up sexually. I know it might sound strange to link your inner child to sexual pleasure, but self-love, self-acceptance, and healing old wounds are keys to living a juicier life. Getting in touch with your inner child and wanting her to delight in life is part of that. Plus, the truth is that most children are sexually curious by nature and tend to find arousal quite easily and accidentally, such as while playing on a rocking horse, and there's nothing wrong with that.

Practice:

NURTURING YOUR INNER CHILD

Think of yourself as a child, your own little baby. Spend some time looking in the mirror or at a baby/toddler photo of yourself, and consider what messages you'd give this child if she were feeling shame, fear, or guilt. What would you say to her?

Now say it to yourself, ideally out loud.

Have a box of tissues nearby, as this just might crack your heart open and result in a flood of tears.

How was that for you? Were you able to see what your little girl wounds are and where you could use more love, kindness, and compassion? Continue to cultivate that relationship with your inner child. Get in touch with your innocence and childlike sense of wonder and enjoyment. Notice how this improves your mood and your relationships over time, and how that affects your food choices. *What are you feeding her?*

Fear of Being Sexy, and How to Feel Safe

There's a polarity many women experience: the simultaneous desire to be desired as well as a fear of unwanted attention that could result in predatory harm. If you don't want to attract attention, if you're afraid of it or protecting yourself from it, then you are likely—unknowingly or knowingly—dimming your light and possibly even putting on extra weight. You're likely to close your heart, shut down part of yourself, and block the energy that wants to flow through you. You're likely to deny yourself your divine birthright to experience the pleasure of sex energy running through you all throughout the day. It's as if maybe you feel you don't *deserve* such delight around the clock! But you do.

Many women have been programmed to feel fearful or ashamed of letting their sexual energy shine brightly and flow freely. There's the fear of being judged, stalked, raped, used, abused, disrespected, shamed, cast out, out of control, and unleashed (even when we simultaneously yearn for that last one).

What's the solution, then? How do we make ourselves feel safe? Packing on the pounds or staying home or dressing down and dimming your light are not healthy solutions. Depending on your past experiences and reasons for feeling fearful, it's possible that EMDR (Eye Movement Desensitization and Reprocessing) or some other sort of trauma therapy would best serve you. You can also have some breakthroughs from journaling practices. Or you could take a self-defense class, work with affirmations, or seek help from a therapist or coach. Another option is to find a women's group or training program that focuses on awakening sacred sexuality and feminine power. All of these are methods that can help you deprogram and reprogram yourself over time, through trial and error and with loving presence and patience.

How Loosening Up Helps You Let Go

Muscular tension can also be a barrier to orgasm because it blocks the movement of energy and blood. If you relax your body, your energy and blood can flow better, which enhances orgasm and pleasure. Plus, when you relax your body, your mind relaxes as well so you can be less in your head and more in the present moment, more in your body—more *embodied*.

Some of my favorite ways to relax muscular tension are:

- massage (self or professional)
- Epsom salt baths
- yoga or stretching
- qigong
- going for a walk
- lying down with or without someone to snuggle
- meditation

Take a moment to think about what relaxes *you*.

What you eat also affects how relaxed or tense you are—physically, emotionally, and energetically. Physically, there are certain foods that contribute to feelings of stiffness and tension by creating or contributing to inflammation or lactic acid build up. There's also the effect of mineral depletion that occurs when eating sugar. If not getting the proper nutrients, our muscle tissue health is affected, and we can experience more tension and pain in the body. Hydration also affects muscle tension. *Are you drinking enough water?*

Also consider that what you eat can affect you emotionally, and your emotions can affect your musculature. Have you ever noticed yourself feeling happier and more relaxed after eating, or more agitated and physically tense? For me, I know that if I eat sugar late at night, I'm likely to wake up feeling anxious. Once I notice the feeling of anxiety, I might tense up physically even more before remembering to use my toolbox of relaxation techniques.

And consider caffeine. What does caffeine do to your body and the energy flow if taken in excess? Jacks it up.

Speaking of energy, yes, sugar and caffeine and drugs will get your energy out of whack, and that can lead to muscular tension, which cuts off energy flow, and then it's a vicious cycle of reaching for foods and stimulants instead of feeling fulfilled and energized naturally. It's harder to *truly* enjoy life and relax into pleasure if feeling controlled by this cycle. It's essential to clean up your diet, to make food choices that support relaxation as well as *healthy and sustainable* energy flow rather than synthetic, short-lived energy bursts such as those coming from caffeine and sugar.

But if you're not ready to cut stuff out of your diet yet, then don't. Just relax; don't worry about it. Now, let's see how relaxed you are in this moment and how relaxed you can be.

Practice:

TENSION INVENTORY & FULL-BODY RELAXATION

You can get out your journal and write your answers to the following questions or just think about them in your head:

- How tense are you right now?

- How tense are you when eating?

- How tense are you when having sex or masturbating or even just naked?

- Where do you feel tension?

- Is your jaw relaxed?

- Is your belly soft?

These are all good questions to ask to bring more awareness. Sometimes simply asking the question triggers a release of needless bodily tension.

You can also revisit the guided full-body relaxation meditation recording from chapter 2 at www.rebeccacliogould.com/bookbonus.

Regardless of the method, relaxing your body and relieving tension, without agenda for it to be sexual or result in orgasm, can help you open up to experiencing more pleasure. If you have difficulty with orgasm or with delighting in life, start with learning how to soften your body, little by little. No pressure. No rush.

Oxytocin, Opening Up, and Slowing Down

Since slowing down is a primary characteristic of the Feminine, learning to slow down helps us connect with and heal our sexuality. Furthermore, rushing depletes oxytocin, the "love" hormone or "cuddle" hormone. When you rush around, your body produces a stress response in which cortisol (the stress hormone) levels rise and oxytocin levels drop. For instance, if sex with your partner, or even with yourself, is rushed, it can be less pleasurable and harder to reach a peak orgasm—unless, of course, the time pressure of a quickie is what gets you off.

If rushing is a problem you face, refer back to chapter 1, and free up more time for sex and masturbation so that you feel less stressed and less pressure to "achieve" orgasm quickly. Slowing down also allows you— and your partner if partnered—to drop deeper into your body and be more fully present for your Sacred Energy Exchange. This sort of deep presence is an aphrodisiac that can enhance sexual energy flow and plea- sure. If you've never experienced a lover being deeply present with you, or if you're not so good at being truly present with yourself, this may not make sense to you. That's okay. As you engage with the practices in this book, you will develop your capacity for true presence and discover that even your own presence with yourself can be a huge turn-on.

Now let's take the example of self-pleasuring in terms of actual masturbation—using your own hands or fingers. I'll share something personal here: I used to have an aversion to "finger fucking." I still do, actually, at least in the way the average man might go about it, as in they go for it right away. *My* yoni doesn't want any form of penetration that comes so suddenly and quickly. My body does not open up to that. And energetically and emotionally, it feels rushed and full of agenda. I noticed years ago that this aversion even applied to the use of my own fingers. And guess what helped me get over that?

That's right; slowing down.

So the following practice is near and dear to me, as for most of my life I didn't want fingers inside of me, not even my own. Why? I wasn't raped or molested, but I experienced more than one traumatic catheterization in the hospital at the age of sixteen. At the time, I was still a virgin and had never even inserted a tampon. Nothing had ever entered my vagina, but there I was being poked and prodded in the hospital. And each time, it sent me into hysterics; if you had heard the way I was screaming, you'd think I *was* being raped or tortured in some other way. Needless to say, it was highly traumatic. And later in life, it made me realize that many women have sexual trauma of which they're not even aware. Sometimes it even comes from watching sexual violence on TV or a movie that imprints and creates fear. If you need professional assistance addressing trauma, please see the Resources section and reach out for help.

Regardless of whether you do or do not have any aversion to fingers, experiment with the practice I call Slowly Entering the Temple.

Practice:

SLOWLY ENTERING THE TEMPLE

You can ask your partner* to do this, and/or you can do it in a self-pleasuring session. If you're partnered, I suggest both—practice with yourself and with your partner.

First, just place one hand (yours or your partner's) over your yoni, cupping her with total gentleness, patience, and presence. And breathe.

Eye-gazing with your partner or with yourself in the mirror as well as nurturing touch on the face or soft kisses are all good at this time, too.

Imagine or feel as if you are breathing in and out through your yoni, while connecting with that hand. Just feel that presence of a warm, loving hand that has no agenda and is going to wait for you to make a move. Allow your yoni to open on her own accord, slowly welcoming in a finger or two, but at first without any movement, no thrusting, no agenda to stimulate or produce an orgasm; just entrance. And then pause and breathe there.

Keep the fingers still and allow your body to start the motion, naturally, along with breath. And slowly, arousal and desire are likely to build. If your partner starts *doing* something, and it makes you start to contract or close, say "stop." Or you can go with it if it feels right. You can also ask for the movement of the fingers in and out instead of, or in addition to, your own movement.

Figure on taking about twenty minutes before any penetration occurs. You may naturally open up to receive penetration sooner, or it may take longer or not feel right at all in this particular session. Just having your hand or your partner's hand over your yoni for twenty minutes can be deeply healing and a step toward greater intimacy and pleasure.

* If practicing with a partner, make it clear that he or she needs to practice restraint if there is an urge to enter before you say you're ready.

Option: Decide in advance there will be no penetration, no "entering the temple." Simply cup the yoni and breathe, focusing on building your sense of connection and intimacy with yourself.

Allowing Arousal

Huh? Could it be that simple? Just a decision to allow?

Sometimes you probably don't allow arousal. Maybe you feel numb or try to suppress or contain it when that feeling comes on because it seems like an inappropriate time or place, such as when driving in your car or receiving a professional massage. Maybe you're worried about offending someone, and you want to respect the other person's boundaries. Or maybe you start to feel aroused but can't go masturbate or have sex, so you shut it off thinking nothing can be *done* about it, or with it, in terms of rubbing your genitals against someone or something. But the truth is there's no need to shut it down or turn yourself off. It's just a matter of learning how to let the energy flow and welcoming the pleasure of arousal and orgasmic energy even if it's not going to lead to sex, masturbation, or peak orgasm. So, let's explore how much you can relax into your state of arousal, how much you can allow it, receive it, and enjoy it; this will also help you practice the Sex Energy Circulation from chapter 2 anytime, even when out in public.

Practice:

AROUSAL ALLOWANCE & AWARENESS

Part 1: This week, I invite you to notice when you might be shutting down or turning off. Sometimes just noticing is enough to make a difference. See if you can allow yourself to feel your arousal without shutting down, even if just for a minute or two if you truly can't ride it out to completion. And enjoy it!

Part 2: Next time you notice that you feel aroused in a "non-sexual" situation, ask yourself these questions in the moment, or reflect on them later:

- Does it agitate you?
- Do you feel ashamed?
- Does it energize you?
- Can you feel both energized and relaxed at the same time?
- And can you love yourself enough to fully open to the delight in your arousal?

This can also be added to your menu plan and done during meal time, while eating. Allow yourself to feel the pleasure and arousal of the food in your mouth, delighting in the taste and the texture.

Practice allowing arousal when out in public, and relaxing into it rather than shutting it down. Let it bring a smile to your face. Let it make you glow. Nobody needs to know why, other than you. Even if just for a moment, practice this allowance. Be grateful for it. And over time, you will find yourself feeling happier and more comfortable in your body and with your sexuality.

Stop Being So Serious

Don't be too serious when it comes to engaging with the practices in this book, or if you feel challenged by any of the material here. Just be easy with it. My Sheng Zhen teacher Master Li always says, "being too serious blocks qi flow." When you're too serious, you're up in your head, totally cerebral, disconnected from your body, and your vital life-force energy isn't flowing. Loosen up and lighten up. I invite you to be playful. Don't be afraid to get messy, to make mistakes, to embarrass yourself. It's okay.

Some of the practices in this book will help you loosen up *and* get in touch with your inner child, which will help you open up to more delight. The more fun you can have and the less of a perfectionist you can be, the more enjoyable life can be. And the more you enjoy life, the more fulfilled you feel. The better you feel, the better your eating habits and other activity choices will be.

Practice:

REMEMBER HOW TO PLAY

Make a list or journal about one or the other or both:

- What are your favorite ways to play?
- In what areas of your life are you being too serious?
- And in those areas, what's one change you can make to lighten up and be more playful and relaxed?

Dealing with Pleasure Anxiety, Childhood Wounds, and Brainwashing

Sometimes being playful and experiencing pleasure is easier said than done. If you were ever scolded as a child in the midst of, or after, doing something fun and pleasurable (whether sexually arousing or not), you may have some "pleasure anxiety." If so, then pleasure may feel out of reach or scary. Pleasure anxiety can also result in you turning to food as a *safe* form of pleasure and as a way to self-soothe.

If you were ever shamed or punished for masturbating, **it's time to take your power back, to reclaim your pleasure and your right to touch yourself and feel sexually satisfied and fulfilled.** It might be hard to believe it's okay. It might be hard to let go if, when you were a child, you were punished or teased for being you, and if you were programmed to believe that you shouldn't touch yourself or that you should sit still or always "be good." And that's why I suggest you practice "being bad."

Practice:

DELIGHT IN "BEING BAD"

This was homework from the Institute for Integrative Nutrition® (IIN®) when I was receiving my Health Coach training. The assignment was to choose a few activities during the week where you could "be bad," be mischievous. For example, pressing all the buttons on the elevator before getting off and right before a bunch of other people get on.

Don't do anything that would actually harm another person or be illegal, but come up with three ways to be bad this week, three things you think you probably shouldn't do. It could be something like calling in sick to work to go to a movie or eating something you normally don't let yourself eat and really delighting in it.

Practice "being bad" in small ways, and learn to replace feelings of guilt and shame with joyfulness, playfulness, and a sense of renewed vitality.

Adapted from an IIN handout © 2012 Integrative Nutrition Inc. (used with permission).

Consider the possibility that you've been shamed and domesticated out of being an enchanted, playful, curious, delightful being. Oftentimes children are delighting in play that may or may not be sexually arousing, and they get scolded right in the middle of it. Were you ever told to sit still or stop what you were doing?

Or perhaps there was abuse—being beaten, yelled at, or both, in the midst of, or because of, doing something fun, playful, creative, or sexual. Or maybe there never was a delightful childhood, or perhaps there was but then tragedy struck or your delight and pleasure and playfulness were conditioned out of you. Even if not abused but just scolded, it's possible to internalize that and think it's wrong, not safe, not okay to play or have fun or touch yourself or allow your body to move how it wants to.

How would you like a clean slate? It doesn't matter what was. You can start fresh today. What's in the past is over now. There may be some stored energy, but the story is an illusion; it's not happening now. It's time to let go. As I've already mentioned, you might need professional help, like hypnosis, EMDR, or SomatoEmotional Release. Or it might just take time, patience, and dedicated self-love and self-care practices.

If you've been brainwashed into thinking that touching yourself is bad or wrong or that you're not sexy, it's time to brainwash yourself to believe the opposite.

Practice:

POSITIVE BRAINWASHING (A.K.A. AFFIRMATIONS)

Affirmations are helpful as long as they don't trigger your subconscious's bullshit meter. What does that mean? That means that if you've been held hostage by negative beliefs for years, you can't just start repeating to yourself the opposite and expect it to work. It's too extreme of a jump.

For example, if you believe you're not sexy or have never felt sexy, don't start saying to yourself, "I am sexy. I am sexy. I am sooooo sexy." Not yet, anyway. Ease into it.

First, use words like, "I desire to feel sexy," "I like the thought of being sexy," or something like, "Even though I don't feel sexy, I love myself." And if loving yourself is tricky or sounds like *BS* to your subconscious, see chapter 5 for the "I intend to love myself" affirmation.

You can also play around with affirmations like these: "I intend to feel guilt-free pleasure when I touch myself," or "I'm learning to believe that there's no shame in sexual pleasure."

Use affirmations throughout the day, particularly first thing in the morning and at night before bed. You can use affirmations along with each breath while meditating or mindfully walking. Affirmations can also be used prior to meals or snacks, or even while eating, along with some mindful chewing.

Feeling Guilty about Feeling Good

Even after all of this, there still might be something stopping you. Do you ever feel guilty about feeling good? Take a moment to ponder this. It might be pretty deeply buried, not obvious. But think about whether—when you were growing up or now as an adult—those around you were down and out or seemed to have it harder than you. Maybe they brought you down, or you didn't want to make them feel even worse by sharing what was good and how awesome you felt, so you dimmed your light. Maybe you don't feel totally worthy of blissful, ecstatic delight. Maybe you don't believe you deserve it, especially when those around you are suffering.

But you know what? If you keep shining your light and shining it brighter and brighter, some of those people around you will start to lighten up and brighten up as well. And even if not? Don't be a martyr. Save yourself. You deserve to be happy. You deserve to feel pleasure. You deserve to experience delight and to delight in your delight. Read that again and soak it in: **You deserve to be happy. You deserve to feel pleasure. You deserve to experience delight and to delight in your delight.**

Remember that guilt serves no purpose unless you've truly done something wrong and need to make amends. And how could it be wrong to be happy and to experience the pleasure your body was built to experience?

Unfortunately, many people in our society don't allow themselves to be as happy as they can be. So as you start showing up happier and healthier, although it can have a positive ripple effect, it can also trigger discomfort or jealousy in others. *You* might even feel uncomfortable at first if it's not the norm for you. But once you get in the habit of feeling good and letting in more pleasure, allowing yourself to truly delight in it, and shining your light as bright as the star that you are, you will be so glad you got through the awkward phase, the phase in which you maybe feel a bit silly or like a phony, or maybe even a little crazy. At this point, it won't matter what you or anyone else thought during the growing pains phase of your transformation because any guilt you used to have for feeling good will be gone. You'll be in touch with your desires and your body, know what and how much to eat, have more energy, and exude a radiant glow.

Rippling Out

Just as I'm encouraging you to allow your pleasure to ripple out in waves through your body all throughout your day, I encourage you to allow others to delight in your delight as well. Rather than feeling embarrassed or like you don't want others to feel uncomfortable or bad, recognize your power in spreading your delight, in being a beacon of light. Think about the ripple effect. The more you can freely and openly feel and express and radiate your own delight, the more hearts and lives you touch, and the better this world becomes for all.

THIS WEEK I INVITE you to make yourself some permission slips and notice when you might be shutting down or turning off. Sometimes just noticing is enough to make a difference. See if you can allow yourself to feel your feelings fully.

In addition to riding out painful emotions, practice more fully embracing the positive emotions. Notice when you feel happy or sexually aroused, be grateful, and enjoy it!

Chapter 5

WHAT'S LOVE
GOT TO DO WITH IT?

*"The true opening of our sexuality is not possible
without the true opening of our hearts."*

~ SHAKTI MALAN

To release blockages to orgasmic pleasure and live a life of unrestrained enjoyment and excitement requires cultivating an open heart and harnessing the pure energy of love. Loving yourself and your body is foundational to achieving your health goals. You really cannot succeed by deciding you won't love yourself or your body until you lose a certain number of pounds or look a certain way. Instead, you need to start by loving yourself and accepting yourself as is, and then, from that place of love and acceptance, you will find it easier to make healthier choices when it comes to what you eat and what you do.

Start with the Heart

In Traditional Chinese Medicine (TCM) as well as in other frameworks such as Tantra (an ancient Indian tradition of beliefs, meditation, and ritual practices for channeling the divine cosmic energy into the human microcosm to attain enlightenment), the Heart is referred to as far more than the organ in your chest that works around the clock to keep your blood flowing. And that is why I'll often be writing the word with a capital "H" from now on. In addition to this physical, blood-pumping role in your vitality, the Heart is also an energy center, an emotional center, an alchemical chamber through which negative emotions can be transmuted and transformed.

According to TCM, when the Heart is open, qi flows, and when qi flows, blood moves. Why does this matter in terms of sexuality and the Multi-Orgasmic Diet? Good circulation is crucial to arousal and pleasure because it enhances engorgement as well as lubrication. The more aware you become of the qi and the pure energy of love circulating through you, the more fully alive you will feel. And *feeling fully alive* can make you feel sexier and more in touch with your capacity for pleasure. Furthermore, in *Tantra: The Path of Ecstasy*, Georg Feuerstein states that awakening the energetic heart center can prevent negative side effects that may arise when focusing on the lower energy centers associated with sexual energy and desire.

There is also a connection between the capacity for love and orgastic potency. The more you open your Heart to give and receive love, while relaxing and opening up to this pure energy of love flowing through you, the more orgasmic you become. And the more orgasmic you are, the greater your potential for heightened arousal, pleasure, and enjoyment, not just genitally, but in all of life.

To live fully alive, you must feel *all* your feelings and have an open Heart through which they can flow. The greater your capacity to feel your feelings, the more you might be affected by the emotional state of those around you. You may feel increased joy and bliss, but you may also experience an increase in pain and sorrow as you soften, open more, and become increasingly sensitive to others. That's why it's beneficial to have some sort of practice that will help you keep the energy, feelings, and emotions flowing freely rather than getting stuck and bringing you down.

Plus, to make any sustainable transformation, having a mindfulness practice is key. A mindfulness, or awareness, practice helps quiet and focus your mind. Examples include meditation, breathwork, mindful walking, even coloring books! It could really be anything to which you bring heightened awareness. Moving your body, and the energy that flows through it, is also crucial to your overall health and well-being. So I have a solution to share with you, a one-stop-shop for Heart-opening along with physical, emotional, and spiritual well-being: Sheng Zhen.

What the Heck is Sheng Zhen?!

As briefly mentioned in chapter 2, Sheng Zhen ("shung jen") is a system of qigong developed by Master Li Junfeng. It is the Qigong of Unconditional Love, and it has a unique focus on opening the Heart as well as the unique characteristic of poetic contemplations, which accompany many of the movements and help you understand life in order to live it more fully. Because of the importance of Love as a basic and original energy of the Universe, I'll now use a capital "L" when referencing this universal Love energy.

Sheng Zhen in Chinese literally means Sacred Truth, which is further defined to mean Unconditional Love. The idea here is that Unconditional Love is the highest, most sacred Truth. And Unconditional Love is a pure energy, an energy that is always with qi.

Sheng Zhen has three primary functions:

- **Physical:** Sheng Zhen strengthens the body by improving circulation, increasing flexibility, and fortifying the immune system.
- **Emotional:** Sheng Zhen relaxes the mind by balancing the emotions and reducing stress, anger, and anxiety.
- **Spiritual:** Sheng Zhen opens the Heart by helping you cultivate compassion, joy, and an understanding of yourself and the world.

Sheng Zhen is more than a type of qigong; it's a way of living a loving life that people of any religion or belief system can incorporate into their current practices. Sheng Zhen covers it all: the Heart, mindfulness and movement, the physical, the emotional, and the spiritual. And since your mind is like a very powerful computer, the poetic contemplations that accompany the movements also help to reprogram your mind's operating system with positive messages and affirmations. A couple of my favorite contemplations express it very well: Sheng Zhen can take you to a state of "bliss at the core" in which you feel the "delight of simply existing."

In addition to strengthening the immune system and helping your physical body, this system of qigong reduces stress, eases anxiety, and helps you overcome blockages and resistance by opening your Heart so that all emotions can pass through freely. Opening the Heart and cultivating the pure energy of Love will help you connect more easily with your soul, your inner wisdom, and this will lead you to make healthier choices in all areas of your life—not only in what you eat but also in your relationships with others and with the environment and society as a whole. Opening the Heart makes it easier to love others and have less conflict.

The Sacred Truth about Love, The Sacred Truth About Sex

Although Sheng Zhen does not teach sexual energy cultivation practices, the *truth* is that opening the Heart is an important part of sexuality. Sheng Zhen's teachings encourage people to relax and enjoy life, and its practices remove stress, which weakens sexual energy. When we develop a deeper sense of connection and oneness with ourselves, others, and the world around us, it is carried over into the realm of sexuality as part of living a healthier, happier, more joyful existence.

And there's another sacred truth: the truth of the divinity of our sexuality. Although Master Li's teachings and practices don't address this directly, I see a very clear correlation between the Sheng Zhen philosophy of living a loving life with an open Heart and my philosophy of embracing our divinity *through* our sexuality and experiencing as much pleasure (sexual or otherwise) as possible. The truth is that we are sexual beings. The truth is that our bodies—especially women's bodies—were built for pleasure; after all, the clitoris is the only body part with the *sole purpose* of pleasure.

Although Master Li doesn't talk about sex in his classes or books, he always talks about enjoying life and living a loving life. Sex and pleasure are undoubtedly a part of that. So because your body is a sacred temple built for pleasure, there's no shame in delighting in it, in showing it off, in touching it or being touched in ways that arouse you. The truth is that your body needs touch and that you need connection. The truth is that you deserve to experience pleasure, to be turned on, and to feel sexually alive and fulfilled.

If you're denying yourself pleasure and cutting off your sexual energy flow, then you're cheating yourself out of the optimal enjoyment of life. If you don't have a partner, your touch and pleasure needs can be met in other ways, some of which are also explored within these pages. If you've temporarily lost your mojo or feel stuck in a rut, engaging in the practices in this book will help you get your groove back.

Qi Flow, Blood Flow, Relaxation, and Arousal

When you relax your body, both energy and blood flow improve. When energy and blood are circulating in a relaxed and open body, a natural response is arousal. Now, this doesn't necessarily mean there will be an urge for sex or orgasmic climax, but there can be a sense of arousal or pleasure.

You might need to think differently about what arousal is, what it feels like, and what it means to you. For example, I've noticed during or after sitting for meditation or practicing Sheng Zhen Gong, I feel happier and more relaxed. Sometimes I even feel sexually turned on, and sometimes it's just that I feel more alive and turned on by the energy flowing through me.

At first, when I'd notice myself feeling sexually aroused during or after practice, I felt like I should shut it down, like it wasn't "appropriate" in that context. But that's exactly part of why I'm writing this book and have made it my mission to help myself and others do away with shame and taboo. Whatever you feel is natural. It's okay. And the more comfortable with arousal you become, and the more aware you are of it as something that can happen frequently throughout your day, the better you will feel.

But you'll also need to understand what to do with this energy, whether to simply let it be there and circulate in a conscious way, or whether it's getting down to business with a lover or with yourself. We don't want this increase in frequency and heightened state of arousal leading to more feelings of being thwarted in your desire to receive sexual gratification. If stirring things up leads to frustration, you're more likely to make unhealthy choices or perhaps give up on engaging in the practices in this book. Cultivating an open Heart can help prevent negative emotions from arising in response to sexual arousal. Instead, you'll be more likely to relax and simply enjoy it or channel it into something creative.

The Link between Heart and Sex

Another reason why the Heart is important in the Multi-Orgasmic Diet is because of the connection between the Heart and the yoni. It's my understanding that opening the Heart helps open the yoni. But can it be the other way around? Can one's Heart be opened through sex? Absolutely. Anything is possible, and we are all different. I personally believe that the foundation of an open Heart makes for healthier sexual encounters, but no judgment, no shoulds. Do whatever floats your boat.

For several years, I focused on this foundation of opening my Heart through the practice of Sheng Zhen, but I wasn't consciously exploring sexuality. I didn't make or feel an obvious connection between the two. But when I discovered the world of sacred sexuality, I realized *that* was the missing link and that they go hand in hand. Realizing this felt sexually empowering. The way I looked at sex changed because I started seeing it as more multi-dimensional. I even saw it as a way to experience a sense of Oneness, or merging with the Universe, that my Sheng Zhen practices aimed for as well.

Even if my partner wasn't on the same page, I found I could channel both sexual energy and Love energy during sex. And if I focused on opening my own Heart and on sending out and receiving Love—not love that was dependent upon the connection with my partner, but the pure energy of Love—I experienced deeper levels of pleasure and more intense multiple orgasms. However, I also found that sometimes I'd resort to using food to fill a void if my partner wasn't meeting me where I was in terms of consciousness and Love energy, or if I was desiring more of the personal type of love and affection connection.

Emotional Well-Being

It's natural to desire love and affection, touch, and sexual gratification. It's actually essential to your emotional well-being that you get those needs met. Unless you're on a spiritual path that involves transcending sensory desires, I consider these basic human needs. But let's say you're not interested in renunciation and living an ascetic life, at least not yet, and instead you do want to feel fulfilled when it comes to touch, affection, and sexual pleasure.

Unfortunately, if you've been deprived of these things for long enough, you might start to deny the truth of what you want and need. Or perhaps it *looks* like these needs are being met, but it's not fulfilling because there's still something missing. Cultivating the energy of Love— along with harnessing sex energy, amping up the self-love, and living life with an open and loving Heart—will help.

When you practice Sheng Zhen, the emotional benefits can be profound. In addition to the positive contemplations working their magic, you will feel better emotionally because of the focus on opening your Heart and exchanging qi with the Universe. When I first started practicing Sheng Zhen, I actually thought I had a brain tumor because I went from having such a dark cloud over me to being this radiant beacon of light! I was concerned because it seemed like such a radical personality change. But the truth was that I was just transmuting negative emotions and unblocking stagnant qi. I was getting back in touch with my original nature, which is to feel joyful, excited, and curious about life.

As you practice Sheng Zhen on a regular basis, your outlook on life and the way you view yourself will change. It may not be as radical a change as mine, but at the very least, you'll feel more at peace and more optimistic. You'll find more joy and love in the simple things, and therefore heighten your ability to experience a multi-orgasmic life in which you feel more energized, excited, fulfilled, and satisfied all throughout your day.

In addition to the positive effects of Sheng Zhen's beautiful contemplations, when you open your Heart and practice these movements, the Heart acts as a sort of purifying device as you move the energy through you. Your negative emotions can be transformed into Love as they flow through the Heart and out of your body. And **the freer you are of negative emotions, the less likely you are to engage in compulsive or emotional eating.**

A good place for beginners to start is with Awakening the Soul, a set of eight simple yet powerful movements accompanied by poetic contemplations. In my experience, I feel the qi is very strong even if I practice only the first three movements of this form. I can feel my Heart relax and my emotions release.

During the first movement, *Opening the Heart,* I feel what can only be described as a sensation of expansion and joy as my Heart opens. And in the second movement, *Love Descends on Me,* I feel myself nourished and empowered as I receive more qi and more Love. In the third movement, *Unraveling the Heart,* I feel a strong energy between my hands and can feel my Heart softening as it transmutes and releases negative emotions. Your experience may be different, but many of my students report similar experiences. You also may recognize that the upcoming practice is similar to the "Feel the Qi" exercise presented in chapter 2, but the qi will feel *much* stronger in *Unraveling the Heart.*

Although it's important to complete the first two movements of Awakening the Soul before moving on to *Unraveling the Heart,* it would be too much to share all three movements—or the entire form— here, so I have chosen to share only the third with you because it's an excellent example of one Sheng Zhen movement as well as one of the contemplations.

Practice:

AWAKENING THE SOUL ~
A FORM OF SHENG ZHEN GONG

Please note: Although it is acceptable for beginners to start with practicing only the first three movements rather than all eight, **it is important to practice the movements in sequence. It's important to practice Opening the Heart and then Love Descends on Me *prior* to Unraveling the Heart.** This helps to prepare the Heart to unravel, first by opening the Heart and then by receiving more qi and Love.

For right now, it's okay to follow along with the instructions given below, and you will see that the position of your hands in front of your chest is the same as in Feel the Qi from chapter 2. But to really feel the power of Unraveling the Heart, when you are ready to practice the movements in sequence, you can watch a video at www.rebeccacliogould.com/video.

UNRAVELING THE HEART
~ 3RD MOVEMENT OF AWAKENING THE SOUL

1. Sit comfortably on the front edge of a chair with your spine straight. Gradually raise your arms out to the sides, palms facing upward and move hands in an arc upward toward each other over your head, palm facing palm. Stop when hands are shoulder-width apart.

2. Bend your elbows, slowly bringing your hands down until hands end up in front of the chest about head-width apart or a little wider. Elbows are slightly wider apart; the arm pits are slightly open. Hold this position for at least three minutes.

3. Keep your body and head upright. Feel your chest expand and open.

4. Keep your shoulders relaxed while leaving some space between your arms and torso.

5. Keep your forearms in a straight line from fingertips to elbow. Do not bend or flex the wrists.

6. Fingers are naturally extended and spread apart but relaxed. Feel like your hands and Heart are huge. Close your eyes and hold the position.

~ Contemplation ~

"The knot in the Heart is the feeling of smallness
That we know as fear, shame, or pain.
It is slowly unraveled, so gently undone,
Setting the Heart free to move once again.
In the silence of the process beneath the feelings of smallness
Within lies a wealth we find and reveal
Our own understanding, compassion for ourselves,
The foundation of a Heart that is healed.
Relax and listen to the stirrings of the Heart.
Be ready for that wave of recall,
When we delight in the pleasure, in the knowledge and treasure,
The freshness, the awakening of the soul."

©2013, The International Sheng Zhen Society Foundation, reprinted and adapted
with permission from Awakening the Soul: A Form of Sheng Zhen Gong, the Qigong of
Unconditional Love. For more on Sheng Zhen and to find videos and other products,
please visit www.shengzhen.org.

Although all Sheng Zhen practices open the Heart and balance the emotions, during Unraveling the Heart, I personally have always felt an extra strong sense of my negativities being purified as they pass through the Heart while I hold this position. However, please remember that this is in the context of first doing the two preceding movements. All of Awakening the Soul and other Sheng Zhen forms can assist you with emotional well-being.

De-Armoring and Feeling Your Feelings

As mentioned previously, one barrier to orgasm and enjoying life to the fullest is emotional armoring. There are things we experience in life that contribute to the buildup of a crusty shell around our Hearts and around our whole bodies, turning our bodies into a kind of armor of muscular tension and rigidity. Opening the Heart, such as through Sheng Zhen, can help you de-armor. Although Sheng Zhen's primary purposes do not explicitly include "de-armoring" or anything regarding sexuality, Sheng Zhen does help you soften and relax your body, and this will help to soften and relax your Heart and your mind, which will then lead to the transformation and transmutation of fear, shame, and pain. You'll fill with more Love and joy, and you'll learn to trust yourself and the Universe. In doing so, you will make conscious and loving dietary and activity choices more aligned with your greatest good.

De-armoring requires you to be aware of your emotions, which happen to affect your eating habits, cravings, and digestion as well. Although I want you to focus more on positive feelings around your eating, health, and wellness in general, I also want you to feel all of your feelings—the good, the bad, and the ugly. Uncomfortable emotions might get stirred up, both through opening the Heart, Unraveling the Heart, and through all this focus on sexuality and pleasure. In addition to practicing Sheng Zhen Gong, the Feeling and Releasing Your Feelings exercise can support you on this path.

Practice:

FEELING & RELEASING YOUR FEELINGS

Step 1. Lie down outside in the grass, belly down. Or if you must, do this inside on the floor, but connect through the floor to the Earth. Turn your head to one side, ear to the ground and arms up in field goal shape with palms to the ground.

Step 2. First, just be with your feelings. Notice them. Don't deny them. Accept them. And let the Earth fully hold you. Feel your body softening and melting into the Earth.

Step 3. Allow your feelings to release into the Earth, and listen for what the Earth has to say to you. Listening to what the Earth has to say to you means just listening for any wise or supportive words that come through; this might be from the Earth or from your higher self.

Option: You can also release into the Earth by lying on your back and feeling everything leave your body through your back.

The Power of an Open Heart and Self-Love

This path of reclaiming your divine right to experience pleasure and feel safe, fully alive, and expressed as a sexual being is a brave one. And there is a link between courage and an open Heart.

When you open your Heart to the true power of Love, and when you love yourself truly, madly, and deeply, you can draw on the courage of your Heart to face your fears, to feel the fear and do it anyway, to get up when you fall, and to keep loving even when you've been hurt. You can find the courage to express yourself authentically, to stop holding back, and to accept and delight in all that is.

Why does it take courage? Because so many of us have been brainwashed and trained, domesticated even, into suppressing our natural instincts and impulses and conforming to society's expectations and the general repression of our society. We fear being judged, shamed, cast out, or attracting harm by being more openly sexual and in touch with our sexuality and pleasure potential.

It takes courage and self-love to love like you've never been hurt and to be a fully expressive sexual being in this world. And when I say "love like you've never been hurt," that doesn't just refer to loving others. It refers to loving yourself and to loving life because chances are you've also felt hurt by yourself and by life in general. I know I have. And once I started feeling more self-love, my relationship with myself, with others, and with life got so much better. And one of the most helpful tools for amping up the love, in addition to Sheng Zhen? The "Intend to Love Like You've Never Been Hurt" mantra.

Practice:

INTEND TO LOVE LIKE YOU'VE NEVER BEEN HURT

Start with committing to one week, but then recommit for another week and another and another with this as your daily mantra: "Today I intend to love like I've never been hurt."

Think of this not only in terms of loving others, but also in terms of loving yourself. Not only will it impact your interactions with others, but it will free up your own innocence, that inner child, that bubble of joy and Love, openness and curiosity.

When you love yourself more, and specifically love yourself like you've never been hurt, you are less likely to hurt yourself through overeating or other habits you'd like to break. Rather, you are likely to treat yourself with more love and respect. Plus, you'll feel happier when you feel in love with yourself and in love with life, so there will be less of an urge to fill up on junky or excess foods.

From Knowing Your Body to Loving Your Body

One way to love yourself is to get to know yourself, internally, and to send Love to all these different parts of you. When you connect with your internal organs and develop an actual loving relationship with them, especially those that are directly related to digestion and elimination, you will find that your eating habits just might change out of a subtle recognition and consideration for the impact of your food choices on those organs.

Practice:

BEFRIENDING YOUR ORGANS

This practice is best done when you wake up in the morning. It can also be done before going to sleep at night.

Step 1. With your eyes closed, bring your attention to your heart. Smile as you picture your heart and take a few deep breaths as you send Love to your heart. You can picture the energy of Love as pink or white light, traveling to and bathing this organ.

Step 2. After a few moments at the heart, continue on to your lungs, stomach, pancreas, gallbladder, liver, kidneys, small intestine, and large intestine, taking a few breaths at each organ and sending Love with each breath. I encourage you to also include your ovaries and sexual organs in this practice.

Advanced Practice Option: Take a few moments to ask each organ, "How are you today? Is there anything I can do to make you happier today?"

This practice was inspired by Mantak Chia's "Inner Smile," which can also be found in the Resources section. Befriending Your Organs is also similar to (and can be combined with) the Orgasmic Organs practice in chapter 3. As you open your Heart and build an intimate relationship with your body, your pleasure potential and orgasmic capacity is likely to increase. So get ready for some phenomenal self-pleasuring sessions in chapter 8. But first, build a foundation to prepare yourself by working on opening the Heart with Sheng Zhen and the other practices in this chapter, while also exploring the pleasure of conscious breathing and heightened senses in the next couple of chapters.

THIS WEEK, START THINKING of yourself as the big body of Love that you are! In addition to the practices above, start using the Sheng Zhen mantra: **"I am a big body of Love; full of qi, full of Love."** Anytime you need a little extra boost of energy or are feeling down, remember that you are full of qi and full of Love. Remember that you *are* a big body of Love.

Let this Love energy fill you up and fulfill you. You just might find yourself smiling and laughing throughout your day for no apparent reason. This is a pleasant side effect of living life with an open and loving Heart. *Enjoy!*

And remember, for more on Sheng Zhen and to find videos, visit www.shengzhen.org.

Chapter 6

THE PLEASURE OF BREATH

"Most of us breathe so poorly
that it is a wonder how we stay alive."
~ SEYMOUR BERNSTEIN

Breath is one of the most important aspects of the Multi-Orgasmic Diet. Breath is life. It's soul food. It helps you relax, open, and drop into your body so that you can feel all the pleasure there is to be felt. Conscious breathing not only relaxes you and reduces stress, but it also enhances your sensory perception, thereby increasing your pleasure potential. Breathing can literally *fill you up* with more energy and a feeling of satisfaction and joy. Breath is one of the most effective techniques I've found for stopping myself from eating something I know I would regret. And how you breathe can make sex or masturbation more, or less, powerful and satisfying.

Before diving more deeply into the pleasure of breath, start with a basic awareness practice.

Practice:

AWARENESS OF BREATH

Take a moment right now to shut your eyes and breathe naturally. And just notice.

Notice how you're breathing:

- Is it shallow or deep?
- Fast or slow?
- Where do you feel it?

No right or wrong answers here. Just noticing. Do this for several breaths or a couple of minutes.

Go ahead; put down this book right now . . . and breathe.

Welcome back. How do you feel? Are you still breathing or did you catch yourself holding your breath? This practice, and these questions, are something for you to come back to over and over again. At first, you'll want to schedule it in or have it on your menu. But over time, it will become a sort of baseline habit when you first sit down to meditate or eat, or when you sit at your desk—whenever it comes to mind. Sometimes you'll remember to do it simply because you'll realize you were holding your breath. Prioritize becoming more aware of this, and over time, you will find that you have more energy, more clarity, and a better outlook in general.

Breathe, You're Alive!

Without breath, there wouldn't be life. Think about it. How long can you hold your breath? There are stories of people who survive without eating. But there are no stories of those who survive without breathing. Breath feeds our brain and blood with oxygen. It's also how we take in more vital life-force energy, or as we called it earlier, qi, and it's this energy that sustains us. Some would say even more so than food.

Even though you breathe all throughout the day, unless you have already been practicing conscious breathing or have done breathwork regularly enough to change your breathing habits and patterns, it's likely that most of your breaths are shallow. You may sometimes, or oftentimes, hold your breath without even realizing it. How did we get so far away from what's natural, from what's so automatic for us as babies? Think about how babies breathe. Their whole body breathes, expanding and contracting with full and continuous breaths; it's as if they are *being* breathed.

You can reclaim this baby-like, natural, full breath by becoming more aware of shallow breaths or breath-holding and taking more conscious, mindful breaths instead. You can learn how to let your entire body breathe again, and in doing so, you will feel more fully alive.

Natural Highs

What are you really after when you're reaching out for sweets or other foods or drinks that make you feel *temporarily* happier? There's more than one answer to this question, but right now, let's look at the desire to feel high, to feel elevated, buzzed, expanded—to feel happier and more alive, uninhibited, free. Your desire to stimulate your pleasure centers.

Well, you don't need to turn to alcohol or drugs or even to food for any of that. Conscious breathing and breathwork can give you a natural high, as can qigong, sex, a good cardio workout, time spent in nature, or masturbation. Breath can make you feel buzzed and blissed out.

When we breathe deeply and consciously, we clean out what's dampening down our ability to feel this vital life-force energy, this sex energy, and our own blood running through us. We also take in massive amounts of both oxygen and qi. All of this creates a natural high. And in Sheng Zhen philosophy, we'd say you're also taking in immense quantities of Love since qi and Love are never separate.

Therefore, a deep and full inhalation is a deep and full taking in of Love. You could even see it as an act of self-love. How much Love can you handle? Are you willing to gift yourself one breath of Love and life after another? Are you truly *willing* to feel more fully alive by breathing life and Love into yourself and opening up to all the pleasure that comes from that? If your answer is yes, then it's simple: commit to a daily conscious breathing practice, whether it's something as basic as a few deep conscious breaths or the Orgasmic Breathing that's coming up soon.

But first, the Opening to Pleasure practice from intimacy coach Kamala Chambers will help you become more aware of how much pleasure can come from the simple act of mindful breathing.

Practice:

OPENING TO PLEASURE

1. Allow yourself to rest alone in a comfortable position.

2. Take slow deep breaths. As you exhale, breathe all the way down your body and into your feet. As you inhale, breathe all the way from your feet up to the top of your head.

3. Consider that there is a wave of energy that comes up from the Earth and pulses all the way up your legs, up your torso, and out the top of your head.

   Now feel that wave moving from your head, down your torso and legs, and out the bottom of your feet. This wave ideally would be a slow, steady pulse like a gentle ocean tide or move like a long steady breath. If your body is constricted, or you shut off parts of you, like your pelvis or your heart, then the wave can't pulse all the way through you.

4. Notice how your body feels. Notice where your body or your breath might feel constricted. What is enjoyable about this experience?

5. Notice what parts of your body have pleasurable sensations. Allow your breath to move into the areas of your body that feel pleasure. Allow your breath to heighten whatever pleasure you're experiencing.

6. Either journal about what you discovered or share with a partner.

© 2014 _Road to Love_ by Kamala Chambers, reprinted with permission.

Feeling naturally high from the pleasure of breath yet? If yes, fantastic! And if not, don't worry. Keep practicing. And keep reading.

Restricted Breathing and Resistance to Life

When I asked in the previous section if you were willing to gift yourself one breath of Love and life after another and to open up to all of the pleasure that comes from that, perhaps you thought "yes." Perhaps you even smiled and said it out loud. But there's a chance that you will, or already do, feel some resistance. Don't worry. It's a common response to the fear that arises when making changes outside your comfort zone. It's also normal to freak out a bit when you start to *feel* more as well as when you realize just how little you may have been feeling before.

During the first minute of certain types of breathwork, many people feel such a strong resistance and discomfort that they want to stop. This tends to happen because there's a fear of, and a resistance to, feeling all that comes up, both when you have to clear out the junk and when you open up to feeling more—more of everything, especially the bliss, the pleasure. It can feel so powerful. And that power can feel scary. *Why?* Because human beings tend to be most comfortable with what they know. They fear the unknowns that come along with change. There may also be a resistance to the extra responsibility that seems to go along with increased knowledge and power.

The breathing practices in this book will not be as demanding or intense as formal breathwork, such as Rebirthing (a technique of consciously connected breathing where there is no pause between the inhalation and exhalation). However, even with less intense breathing practices, you may feel resistance. If you do, simply practice breathing through it and letting it go each time you exhale. The Yes Breath, on the following page, will help with this.

Practice:

THE YES BREATH

When you notice yourself feeling stuck, feeling resistance or fear, take a deep, conscious breath in and think of that inhalation as a "yes" to life. Exhale out the fear or resistance or whatever is holding you back. This is easy to incorporate into your life as needed. Sometimes one breath is all it takes to reset. Sometimes you might need more.

When feeling resistance, you may notice a tendency to reach out for sweets or other foods. Therefore, this is also a helpful practice for intercepting cravings. Taking a conscious, life-affirming breath just might stop you from giving in to an unhealthy craving or at least help you eat less junk food—or as I prefer to call it, "comfort food."

In conscious breathing, and in many forms of breathwork, we are saying "yes" to life when we inhale. And on the exhalation? We let go and release what no longer serves us. As you bring this symbolic awareness to your breath, you'll find yourself making healthier choices more naturally. As you consciously affirm life with each breath, you will be drawn more to what is good for you, and less to what is not.

The Pleasure of Expansion

In *The Function of the Orgasm*, Wilhelm Reich explains that, scientifically, expansion and pleasure go hand in hand. When you relax, there's a sense of expansion, and even sometimes a sense of relief from contraction. When you're relaxed, qi flows better, and when this energy is circulating more fully you experience a heightened sense of expansion or spaciousness, which can be highly arousing because your blood flows more freely and can stream more easily to your erogenous zones.

What does this have to do with breath? It has to do with finding the pleasure of simply taking a breath. When you inhale, your lungs expand. The slower and deeper we breathe, the more we expand our lungs. And when you slow your breath, your body relaxes, thereby also relaxing your mind. This all results in the capacity to experience more pleasure, whether during lovemaking, enjoying a meal, or simply sitting and breathing mindfully.

As you fine-tune your ability to relax your body and feel the energy flowing inside you, you will experience a sort of internal massage or caress. Consider the practice of Sheng Zhen, the Heart-opening Qigong. When your Heart is open, there's a sense of expansiveness. If you allow yourself to drop your attention down into your pelvis or your heart, you can feel the arousal that comes with an open-hearted expansiveness. Taking conscious breaths and learning how to direct your breath to various parts of your body will allow you to feel even more expansiveness and pleasure, along with an extra boost of energizing oxygen and qi.

Types of Breath

There are many different breathing techniques, and each can affect the nervous system and, therefore, affect your mood and overall sense of health and well-being. In the yogic tradition, breath control is called *pranayama*. *Prana* is energy, like qi. But terminology aside, the most basic types of breath are belly breathing and chest breathing, deep breathing and shallow breathing, and breathing in through the nose versus breathing in through the mouth. The following practice will help you explore some of these variations.

Practice:

PLAY WITH YOUR BREATH

Sit comfortably, and after each of the following techniques, assess how you feel physically, emotionally, mentally, and energetically. Also take note of which types of breath allow you to take the longest inhalation. Count as you inhale and exhale and notice any differences in the length of each.

With each inhalation, see if you can relax into feeling the pleasure of breath. See if you can feel the breath caressing you from the inside. You may notice that with one type of breath, there is a feeling of pleasure or arousal, whereas with another there is not. Be aware of whether there is a feeling of deeper relaxation or pleasure when you exhale.

1. Inhale through your nose while focusing your attention on your belly. Feel or imagine your belly getting round, as if you're blowing up a balloon inside of it. Exhale through your nose. Repeat three times.

2. Inhale through your nose while focusing your attention on your chest, as if trying to expand your chest with your breath. Exhale through your nose. Repeat three times.

3. Inhale through your mouth, focusing your attention on your belly, again trying to round out your belly. Exhale through your mouth. Repeat three times.

4. Inhale through your mouth, focusing your attention on your chest, again trying to expand your chest. Exhale through your mouth. Repeat three times.

The above practices are here primarily to help heighten your awareness of these various ways of breathing and how they feel differently from one another as well as to start introducing the pleasure potential of breath. This practice also may be used prior to a meal or snack or when a craving comes on. You can use it in its entirety, or you may choose just one or two types of breath. Sometimes you will find that rather than a snack, you just needed to breathe. Taking some **mindful breaths can intercept cravings** by helping to calm your system, refocus your mind, and nourish your cells with oxygen and qi. You might even notice that simple, conscious breaths sexually arouse you as they help you drop down more deeply into your relaxed, feminine softness.

The Importance of Fresh Air

Consider doing the above practice outside, or just go for a walk each day. Getting a daily dose of fresh air will serve you well. Walking around your neighborhood certainly has benefits, but research shows that spending time in nature has greater vitalizing effects. But do you really need science to tell you that? Consider how you feel after a walk or hike in the woods or along the beach. Do you feel refreshed? Inspired? Happier? As Richard Ryan, researcher and professor of psychology at the University of Rochester, says, "Nature is fuel for the soul. Often when we feel depleted, we reach for a cup of coffee, but research suggests a better way to get energized is to connect with nature."

When we take in more energy through qigong, conscious breathing, and time spent outside, we become less dependent upon food as an energy source. **When you approach meals or snacks from a place of already feeling energized, it will be easier to eat less and to make healthier choices.** Even if all you can do is walk around the block for a few minutes each day, do that. Or open a window and take a few deep breaths. Find a way to connect with nature, ideally daily, even if just for a few minutes. The longer, the better. Going for a walk close to home or your office for even just ten minutes will make a big difference in how you feel. Consider trading out a coffee break for a walk-around-the-block break. Or at least go for a walk while drinking that coffee. Allow the fresh air to cleanse and revitalize you.

Orgasmic Breathing

Now, imagine if you could feel the rush and excitement of sex just through a simple breathing technique. My favorite and most effective way to perk myself up, and also to intercept unhealthy cravings, is to take *orgasmic breaths.* What's an orgasmic breath, you ask? Follow the instructions or bonus video to find out.

Practice:

ORGASMIC BREATH

This is one of the easiest, shortest, and most impactful practices within this book. It's an open-mouthed inhalation that's like a pleasurable gasp. It's similar to the way you might breathe when being passionately and pleasurably thrust into.

1. During the open-mouthed inhalation, feel the air come into the back of your throat.
2. Let the exhalation come out through your mouth as well.

Allow there to be some sound with it. Allow your mind to fantasize, or just be fully present with the breath and the reality of the present moment.

Use three to ten breaths when a craving comes on, before a meal, or just for a pick-me-up. Try it. And visit www.rebeccacliogould.com/bookbonus for your free bonus video demonstration.

Unless it really doesn't feel right for you, I highly recommend adding this to your menu and creating a contract. Post a reminder on your fridge or anywhere that would be helpful. Consider setting reminders in your phone.

This practice is easy to do anytime, anywhere. If you can take ten breaths, great. But it can also take as few as three to make a difference. One day I used just a few Orgasmic Breaths while walking down the street looking at flowers. Why? I was feeling a bit tired and down, too in my head. Then I noticed some flowers and decided to experiment with breathing them in—and doing it in this "orgasmic" way. And it worked! It energized me, perked me up, and made me smile. I encourage you to experiment with this breath on a daily basis. Clients have reported back to me that this breath helped them reduce their compulsive chocolate consumption by over forty percent, which helped them enjoy the chocolate that they *did* eat even more.

Directing Your Breath for Heightened Pleasure

In addition to the Orgasmic Breath, one way to give yourself a little sex energy boost, arouse yourself, and make yourself smile is by breathing into your nipples. When I do this, I don't imagine breathing in *through* my nipples, although that's certainly a practice you could do, but I breathe in through my nose and down into my nipples. I feel the breath going down into my breasts, creating a pleasurable pulsation in the nipples along with the inhalation and exhalation. If you're not used to breathing into various parts of your body, be patient with yourself and use your imagination to picture light or some other visual image for oxygen, qi, and Love moving through you. Trust that your breath and these energies will go where your attention goes.

If this practice feels edgy for you, it's okay to ease into it with a single breath. Or start by breathing into your breasts in general and focusing on Love energy, and then, over time, focus in on your nipples, amping up the sexual energy. In addition to nipple breathing being a self-pleasuring pick-me-up you can use at any time throughout your day, it will also increase your breast and nipple sensitivity. Over time, you may discover that you can even orgasm through nipple play. Yes, that is actually possible and usually requires some real dedication. But for now, just breathe.

Practice:

BREATHING INTO YOUR NIPPLES

Focus your attention on your nipples and inhale slowly through your nose. Feel your chest and your breasts expand and fill with oxygen, qi, and the pure energy of Love. Allow a sense of expansion and arousal. See if you can feel a little tingle in your nipples. And as you exhale, keep your focus on your nipples. Inhale through the nose, and for an extra dose of pleasure-enhancing relaxation, exhale through your mouth with a sigh.

You can add a smile as part of the practice—if it doesn't already occur naturally. Smile at your breasts as if you're saying hello and sending them Love; smile at how silly you feel doing this, or smile in sheer delight of the pleasure of this practice.

Depending on your sensitivity, even just a few of these breaths can work wonders. Sometimes all it takes for me is one, but then it feels so good I want to keep going.

What I advise in the beginning is to set a timer for just three minutes. Heck, you can even set a timer for only one minute. And, of course, you're welcome to set it for five minutes or get rid of the timer altogether and just ride it out for as long—or as short—as you like.

Another option is to start with just three to five of these breaths. This practice can be done while you're in the shower or getting dressed if you're short on time or not ready to give it your full and undivided attention.

Variation: You can also breathe into your yoni. And again, it can be a specific point, such as the clitoris.

___

You can also play around with the pleasure of breathing in various smells and breathing the delight of that smell all the way down into your yoni. And again, if this doesn't feel comfortable for you, you'll still benefit from just allowing yourself to delight in the smell without bringing it all the way down into your body.

Practice:

BREATHING BEYOND THE NOSE, BEYOND THE LUNGS

Sniff a rose or other flower, or anything really, all the way down into your yoni. The idea here is to go deeper than the initial joy you feel in smelling a flower or anything fragrant; take it all the way down through your body, through your core, to your yoni.

To direct your breath, you can think of it as an offering or infusion of Love to this sacred space within you. Let it tickle you and delight you deep inside, all the way down in your sex center.

If you don't *feel* the breath going anywhere other than your nose, chest, or belly, that's fine; just *picture* it. You can visualize the oxygen, qi, Love, and the scent you're taking in as light or incense smoke. Picture it traveling through your body.

Learning to direct your breath to various parts of your body will serve you well, both in and out of the bedroom. If there's a part of your body that feels tense and needs to relax more, you can breathe into it and release the tension as you exhale. If you want to feel more pleasure in any part of your body, directing breath to those parts will heighten the pleasure. And breathing into your belly can help you feel more full and satisfied before or during a meal. If this doesn't make sense to you yet, do your best to keep an open mind and practice the power of creative visualization. Remember, where your attention goes, the qi will follow; this applies to breath, too. After all, breath and qi are intrinsically linked, and that one literal translation of qi *is* breath.

Overeating and Restricted Breathing

Have you ever overeaten and then felt uncomfortable afterward? For example, just when you'd had enough at a holiday meal, someone brought out another side dish or dessert, or your grandma or mother-in-law insisted you eat more. And you went from enjoying yourself and the food and feeling pretty good to feeling lethargic and like you just might burst.

Part of that discomfort is because when you eat too much it's harder to breathe. I find this to be the case both in a physical way, like there's not enough room for my lungs to expand, and in another way. What's this other way? Denial or resistance. Not wanting to feel. If you overeat and then take a deep breath, you have no choice but to feel the discomfort. And, sure, sometimes what we feel is satisfaction, but typically, breathing deeply into an over-stuffed belly feels uncomfortable physically, emotionally, mentally, and even spiritually.

If you stuff yourself full of food, there is less room for you to take full inhalations. Physically, eating too much or eating foods that bloat you can result in the diaphragm moving up into the chest area, thereby crowding the lungs. Emotionally, maybe you feel guilt or shame, a yucky kind of feeling. Mentally, there are thoughts about how much you just ate, again guilt, shame, or some sort of judgment and evaluation. And spiritually? There's a dampening down of energy and a feeling of being out of alignment with your greatest good.

How can you remedy this? Awareness is the first step. And mindful breathing or chewing can be used as your awareness practice here, as they both can help. Begin by noticing how deeply and fully you can breathe before a meal. Taking your time and chewing thoroughly not only prevent overeating, but you'll also experience a sense of fullness without finding it difficult to take a deep breath at the end. By connecting to your breath throughout the dining experience, you'll eat more slowly, experience more pleasure, and still feel nice and satisfied when finished.

Practice:

SAVE ROOM FOR BREATH

Connect with the bliss of breath before eating. Sitting comfortably, close your eyes and take at least three deep breaths. Before each one, notice the air coming in through your nose. See if you can feel a sort of tickle inside your nostrils. And can you feel your breath continuing down through your windpipe, internally massaging your throat?

Notice your body softening and relaxing with each breath. Allow your breath to nourish each and every cell and to fill you with the feeling of love and pleasure. Seal that good feeling in.

Then open your eyes, or keep them closed, as you start eating. Try to maintain that same or similar sense of fullness and ease you were just feeling while breathing.

Before getting to a point of no longer being able to feel as good and light and free with your breath, stop eating. Instead of saving room for dessert, save room for breath. Deep and easy, pleasure-filled, energizing, relaxing breaths. Yum!

By breathing deeper, taking fuller breaths, and being able to consciously control your breathing, you'll have more energy and eat less. You'll also make healthier choices and experience more pleasure. Additionally, as you'll see in the next chapters, conscious breathing will also heighten your sensuality and enhance your self-pleasuring sessions.

IF YOU HAVEN'T ALREADY started taking Orgasmic Breaths prior to meals or snacks or when a craving comes on, start now. Sign a contract. Do this often, and you will get results. Access your book bonuses for a video that clarifies how this practice is done. You can also see another sample menu with practices that you've learned up to this point at www.rebeccacliogould.com/bookbonus.

Also become more aware this week of when you're holding your breath, such as when focusing on typing an email or when driving in traffic or having a difficult conversation. Work on breathing continuously, in and out and in and out in any and all situations.

Play with sending breath to various parts of your body. You can picture your breath as light traveling through you, lighting up whatever part it reaches.

Most importantly, allow yourself to delight in simply breathing, in simply being.

Chapter 7

AWAKENING THE SENSES

"Over time you'll find the answers within your own five senses."
~ VICTORIA ERICKSON,
RHYTHMS & ROADS

When you feel satisfied by various means of healthy sensory stimulation, you'll fall in love with life by connecting more deeply to your surroundings, and you will experience an abundance of fulfillment and delight. Your tendency to numb out or feel lackluster will be replaced by the ability to feel turned on by something like the tickle of a breeze or the lush greenery of the trees. Your desire to fill yourself with junky or excessive foods, activities, or people will diminish. You'll feel happier, make more nourishing choices, and exude a radiant glow. Awakening the senses makes life richer and more enjoyable, pleasurable, and more interesting.

Whether you're eating, having sex, masturbating, or just going for a walk, you'll benefit from getting more intimate with *all* of your senses as it will help you derive deep joy and pleasure from the simplest of things. Most of the practices in this chapter are easy to incorporate throughout your day on a regular basis, and I highly recommend making a commitment to focus your attention on one or more of the five senses for at least the next seven days. Pay attention to how this affects your mood and your eating habits.

Now, are you ready? Let's begin awakening the senses, one by one, and then we'll put them all together at the end of this chapter.

What You Touch

Have you ever delighted in the tactile experience of touching a fuzzy leaf or lightly running your fingers over the ridges of a salt shaker? Or how about gently caressing your cheek with flower petals? Lightly tickling your fingers against the spine of a book or its pages? Or running your fingers through your own hair?

Our sense of touch is an obvious one when it comes to pleasure. At least when it comes to forms of sexual intimacy, such as the feel (and sometimes friction) of skin against skin and being caressed, licked, sucked, or rubbed. But what about the pleasure that comes from feeling an ordinary object in your hands or against other parts of your body? What about the sensation of your clothes or sheets against your skin?

Becoming more aware of the ways in which you can receive tactile satisfaction will help you fill your cup when it comes to touch. Although receiving touch from others is important to your well-being, the more ways you have to meet your own touch needs, the better you'll feel with or without the involvement of others.

One way of increasing your sensitivity—and therefore plea-sure—was shared with me by sex coach and intimacy expert Dr. Betty Martin. Try my adapted version in the Pleasure in the Palms of Your Hands practice.

Practice:

PLEASURE IN THE PALMS OF YOUR HANDS

Gather up several small objects of different shapes, textures, and sizes. Put them into a bag or a hat and then, with eyes closed or blindfolded, take out an item.

You can start by holding it and applying what you learned in chapter 6 to "breathe in" the energy of this object. Or you can start by tracing it with your finger(s). You can use one hand to rub it or glide it around on the other hand. You can pet it. Just explore this item with your hands however you wish.

Breathe naturally. Relax. How does it *feel*? Focus on feeling, but if thoughts arise, notice what they stir up for you, physically and emotionally.

If you can let yourself forget about time, to more deeply sink into feeling each item, go for it. However, if you prefer more structure, go ahead and set a timer for one or two minutes (or more) per item.

Tip: You can also do this with just one item, randomly, throughout your day; it doesn't need to be an event. You can do it with this book right now or with your pen, a salt shaker in the kitchen, a bar of soap in the shower, the steering wheel of your car (but with your eyes open!), etcetera. I took a moment just now to do it with the mouse I've hooked up to my laptop—a thirty-second pleasure break in the midst of work! You can do it. Anytime. Anywhere. With anything.

When you begin to explore your body's ability to respond to touch and pleasure, don't be shy. Really allow yourself to feel turned on sexually—feel your body soften and surrender as you notice a pulsation in your yoni, the quickening of your heart rate, a smile on your face, your chest swelling with each breath. If you need to imagine a lover is tracing the item over your skin, go ahead. And over time, you'll be able to feel aroused simply by what *is* rather than by a fantasy. You'll be able to relax into enjoying the fact that you're the one pleasuring yourself—and in such unconventional ways!

Now, what about touch when it comes to food? There's something quite sensual about getting playful and primal by eating with your hands. It can help you feel more connected to your food as well as to your body—more specifically, to your *animal* body. Why is this important? Because animals have no sexual shame. Animals don't inhibit their sexual energy flow. When you get more in touch with the animal you are and relax into your body, your sexual energy can flow more freely. You'll feel sexier and more alive, perhaps even a bit naughty but in a very good way.

Practice:

PLAY WITH YOUR FOOD

Step 1. Wash your hands well so that you have no excuses here. Use at least one food item, but a variety or a whole meal is even better.

Step 2. Closing your eyes, or leaving them open, use your fingers to pick up your food. Focus on what it feels like in your hands. Feel the texture. Feel the hardness or the softness. Trace it with your fingers, allowing it to tickle your skin.

Step 3. And then feed yourself as if feeding a lover—remember, you *are* your own lover. So feed yourself, and then? Then lick your fingers. This carries over into the sense of taste, of course, but here focus primarily on how it *feels* to your fingers to be licked. Also notice how the food feels inside of your mouth.

When you eat with your hands and treat a snack or meal as if it's part of foreplay with yourself or with life, chances are you will slow down and eat less. Of course, you might find yourself eating ravenously if a sort of passion and desire to devour takes over. But you're still likely to eat less and derive more pleasure and fulfillment as you get more in touch, literally, with your food.

What You Smell

The smell of a lover and of your own self, the smell of food, the smell of sex—all of these smells have the power to affect you, to arouse you. Many smells are neutral, and we don't really notice them. But think about how often a smell is either obviously offensive or obviously pleasing. What smells turn you on? What smells turn you off?

Our sense of smell strongly influences how we feel, especially whether or not we feel turned on. Certain smells are known to be aphrodisiacs, and they differ depending on whether you're male or female. Here's a list of euphoric-inducing scents for men:

- vanilla
- licorice
- cinnamon
- orange
- chocolate
- lavender
- jasmine

And for women, common aphrodisiacs include:

- orange
- jasmine
- rose
- ylang ylang
- licorice
- sandalwood

If you want to feel more relaxed, joyful, and sexy, try using essential oils in a diffuser for aromatherapy. It's an effective way to get the scents into your system, creating actual changes in the brain to bring about a shift in emotion.

We don't want to overuse essential oils to cover up our own scent, though. It's important to get in touch with and feel comfortable with your own natural aromas. In addition to playing around with essential oils and aromatherapy, take some time to smell your own scent.

Practice:

SCENT OF A WOMAN

Part A: Smell yourself. Bury your nose into your wrist or back of your hand and take a big whiff, as if your life depended on it. Shut your eyes and breathe in your scent.

Part B: Smell your yoni. Reach down and touch yourself, whether internally or externally, and then bring your hand back up to your nose.

Yes, that's right. I want you to smell yourself "down there." I want you to smell your sex, smell your yoni. *Yikes!* Right? If you're not already super in touch with your lady parts and completely comfortable with your sexuality, this might be edgy for you. It's important, though. It's not only part of engaging your senses; it's part of self-knowledge and self-love.

Discover a fondness for your own scent, and also notice when you don't smell so good because it can be a sign of an imbalance or infection. Start getting more familiar with how your scent changes depending on diet and other factors—such as if you've taken on a new lover or where you are in your menstrual cycle if still ovulating. You'll feel sexier and more confident if you do.

Allow yourself to delight in the scents of others. Breathe in the scent of your loved ones when hugging or snuggling. Take the scent down into your belly and fill yourself with the joy of connection. Or if this other person smells *bad*, notice whether or not that turns you off or doesn't really matter to you. Just become more aware. Apply this to eating as well.

Practice:

SMELL YOUR FOOD

Sometimes it's easier to tap into our sense of smell when we close our eyes. Start experimenting with smelling your food. Take a few conscious breaths, inhaling the aroma through your nose and breathing it in both before and during your meal. Notice the subtle smells of foods we don't usually think of as being aromatic, such as pumpkin seeds or carrots. Everything smells like *something*, even if it's difficult to detect at first.

Whether your food smells good, bad, or neutral, allow this to be part of your dining experience as a way to make it richer. Be aware of foods that stir up memories or emotions because of their smell. Sometimes this can help you realize why you're drawn to eating something that's not so good for you. For example, maybe your grandmother used to make fried chicken for you, and so you associate this food with feeling loved and nurtured. Ask yourself what else makes you feel loved and nurtured, whether it's eating something healthier, taking a bath, calling a friend—or visiting your grandmother if she's still alive.

As you get in touch with your sense of smell, you'll notice yourself delighting more in what smells good, allowing the scent to be part of what fills you up and brings you joy. You'll also come to realize the power and influence scents may have over you in terms of your cravings. And remember that using aromatherapy can also help enhance positive emotions and feelings of satisfaction, thereby diminishing unhealthy cravings.

Now take a moment to shut your eyes after reading this paragraph, before reading the next section. With your eyes closed, breathe in through your nose, and notice what you smell. If you're somewhere that has no particular smell in the air, decide whether you like that or would like to spice things up a bit by using essential oils to create a more sensual atmosphere. There's no right or wrong here; it's merely an option. See the Resources section for more on aromatherapy.

What You Taste

Mmmm . . . The sense of taste is perhaps the most obvious sense to address when talking about diet, right? When it comes to what we eat, many of us are slaves to our taste buds, at least to some extent. So, what tastes do you crave? What tastes do you like or dislike?

As you become more conscious of the subtleties of taste, eating mindfully, and allowing yourself to more fully take in and enjoy the pleasure you derive from certain flavors, you'll eat less and feel more fulfilled. One of the best ways to get in touch with enjoying taste more fully is to eat with your eyes closed. Give it a shot.

Practice:

EATING WITH YOUR EYES CLOSED

That's it. Plain and simple. Eat with your eyes closed for as often and long as you can, whether it's only for a bite or two or for the entire meal or snack. You're likely to breathe and eat more slowly and notice more flavor.

You will have a chance to go deeper into the subtleties and pleasure of sensuality and taste when eating with your eyes closed later in the chapter. But first, I want you to explore how *you* taste.

Practice:

TASTING YOURSELF

You have a few options here, and I encourage you to explore them all:

1. French kiss yourself. Shut your eyes and get comfortable, ideally lying down or leaning back in a comfy chair, but it can also be done standing, perhaps when you stand in front of your fridge or are grocery shopping. Move your tongue around slowly and seductively, exploring the inside of your mouth. This also doubles as a feeling exercise. So let yourself *feel*, of course, but also focus on the taste. How do you taste? Swallow it down.

2. Lick yourself. Anywhere and everywhere you can. How do you taste?

3. You can set out to do this as its own practice, combine it with a self-pleasuring practice, or do it during sex with a partner. Next time you get wet, reach down and touch yourself if you aren't already, and then bring your fingers back up to your mouth and taste yourself. If you're with a partner, you can also experience your taste on his or her lips after receiving oral sex.

If you think it's gross to taste yourself, or if it feels strange to you to do these practices, that's okay. You're not alone. Accept where you are with self-compassion. You also may want to revisit chapter 4 to take a look at feelings of shame and chapter 8 for an extra dose of self-love. See if you can give yourself permission both to get more intimate with yourself and also to feel discomfort in doing so. As you give yourself permission, giving space to your resistance, you'll begin to ease your way deeper and deeper into these practices. And as you do so, you will deepen your relationship with yourself and feel empowered as a sexy, sensual woman.

What You See

Some say the eyes are gateways to the soul. The more you feed your soul through looking at obviously beautiful things or finding beauty in the mundane, the more content and nourished you will feel.

And unless your vision is severely impaired, it's likely that the most noticeable and primary way you take in information is through your eyes. When we look at food or at a person, what we see will often either turn us on or turn us off. But what if you were to become more aware of this with *everything* you look at?

We are visual creatures and spend a lot of time blankly staring at a screen or at other things in our lives, not really consciously allowing what we see to penetrate or fulfill us. However, there is such a feast that awaits your eyes once you start becoming more receptive and aware— the various greens of trees, the bright pinks and yellows of flowers, the soothing blues of sky and sea. **Your life will feel more vibrant and juicy when you truly open your eyes to see all the beauty that surrounds you.**

Below, you will discover how to drink this beauty through your eyes like a potion, an elixir, or a health tonic that will light you up and make you glow. Your eyes really do have the power to bring you tremendous amounts of pleasure, especially when you combine conscious breathing with conscious gazing. What do I mean by that? I mean that you can amplify the impact of sights—and of any sense—by taking in a breath along with the sensory stimulation. Inhale what you see, breathing it in through your eyes. So let's play a little game with sight, breath, and direction of energy.

Practice:

PENETRATIVE, RECEPTIVE, & NEUTRAL GAZE

Part A: You can look at anything, but I encourage you to combine this with eye-gazing with *yourself* in the mirror. Here's what you do:

- Look into your eyes (or at an object), and at first, just notice. Do you feel neutral, or do you feel some sort of pull forward or push back? Soften your belly and breathe to help you notice what you feel.

- Next, come into a neutral gaze if not already there. If you're not sure what neutral is, don't worry; you'll figure it out as we go along through comparison. With the neutral gaze, you don't take anything in, or send anything out, through your eyes.

- Now imagine your eyes are like a vacuum, or like you're a seductress trying to lure a lover to you. One of the primary essences of feminine energy is to be receptive, and the more you can cultivate the characteristics of feminine energy, the better your sexual energy will flow. You can also think of your eyes like a well, bringing in water, down, down, and down into the core of your body. Really imagine or feel as if you're magnetizing to you and drinking in what you're looking at.

- Then go back to neutral. And from a neutral place, switch to a more penetrative gaze. Imagine you have laser beams for eyes, or like you're on the prowl, hunting down some prey. Do you feel the difference? Do you feel energy moving more forward and outward through your eyes?

Part B: Now that you've practiced the foundation, go for a walk. Let your eyes be like a vacuum, taking in the energy of the trees, the flowers, the leaves, the grass. Occasionally shut your eyes, savoring the sights and the feelings you're feeling, smiling, breathing it all down into your body, particularly down into your yoni and into your heart. Feel for a sense of relaxation and expansion as you nourish yourself visually.

Tip: This is a good practice to do when you're feeling a craving or prior to a meal. Go outside, even if just walking around your neighborhood, and see how much you can fill up on what you see.

You can also practice the direction of energy gazing when with a partner or when looking at people you find attractive. Both men and women are turned on by visual cues, so rather than feeling shameful and suppressing it or trying to pretend you're not aroused, allow yourself to be delighted and titillated by what you see, even if there's nothing to be done about it by engaging with that other person.

The more tuned in you are to the connection between your eyes and your capacity for arousal, the more pleasure there is to tap into and the more easily you can find joy and pleasure purely by looking around, looking in the mirror, or looking at anything. Allowing yourself to fill up on visual stimulation is likely to help curb your cravings and reduce your tendency to overeat or use food to create a sense of fulfillment.

What You Hear

Now it's time to give your eyes a rest, shutting them as you focus more on tuning in to what you hear. But don't shut them yet. First, continue reading. You'll get to shut your eyes soon.

In addition to being housing for what allows us to hear the vibrations that create sound, ears are also a primary erogenous zone. And because they are directly linked to the brain and nervous system, disturbing sounds, or noise, can disrupt and negatively impact nervous system functioning, causing anxiety. In my experience, this can lead to making ungrounded, unhealthy choices, such as excessive or unhealthy eating.

As you know, slowing down is one of the essentials of living a multi-orgasmic life, and it comes into prominent play as we explore all of the senses, but especially the sense of hearing. Why? Because slowing down in loud environments, especially in noisy restaurants or at crowded social events, might prevent you from making unhealthy food choices in these situations. Can you recall being at a restaurant or party that was really loud? Do you remember how you felt? How you ate? How *much* you ate?

Depending on your personality and nervous system, you might be like me: I get easily overstimulated and stressed in loud places. Prior to becoming more conscious of this, when I'd be at noisy restaurants or parties, my tendency would be to eat more quickly (and often in larger quantities) and not always select the best foods.

Clearly, I was feeling anxious and resorting to self-soothing and self-medicating. Instead of slowing down, I would speed up, as if in a rush to consume whatever would numb me out. And it's common for people to knowingly or unknowingly self-medicate and self-soothe overstimulation by stuffing their mouths and bellies to stuff down and suppress feelings of discomfort and stress. Becoming aware of this tendency is the first step to overcoming it. If you think how you eat is affected by noise, or even if it's not, try the Hearing Music Everywhere practice.

Practice:

HEARING MUSIC EVERYWHERE

The next time you're in a loud atmosphere and there's food involved, make a conscious effort to slow down. To breathe more slowly and deeply. To chew more. And to choose your food wisely. You can also choose to put in ear plugs or to leave and go somewhere with more peace and quiet! Or you can practice imagining that all that *noise* is actually a beautiful symphony.

A symphony? Yes, a symphony rather than a cacophony. See if you can take in obnoxious background noise as more of a symphony of sound. It just might help you enjoy the noise rather than being irritated or stressed by it.

Allow your ears to be receivers for all sorts of pleasurable surprises, and notice how it affects your mood and your appetite. Consider devoting a day to listening, to hearing. And find the music within: the buzz of the lawn mowers, the chirps of the birds, the rush of the water as you wash the dishes. Open up your ears to the beauty, the music, in all sounds for the day.

And take it all in with a smile. That's an important part of this. Don't just hear it mechanically; breathe it in, drink it in, swallow it down, and smile. Let yourself feel filled up, lifted up, and delighted by even the most ordinary and familiar sounds.

Just like drinking in the sights through your eyes, drinking in the sounds through your ears is a way to experience more pleasure and joy and, therefore, feel more fulfilled throughout your day.

Now that we've looked at ambient noise as music, how about some *actual* music, some *orgasmic* music? Have you ever noticed that some songs turn you on, whether because of the sultry lyrics, the vibration of the bass line or vocals, or the combination of it all? Within some songs, there is only one obvious climax. Some have multiple climaxes. But if you listen closely, all music is multi-orgasmic, though some songs more obviously so than others. So pay attention from now on to the music to which you listen. Where's the buildup? Where's the release? Can you feel it in your body?

Practice:

GOOD VIBRATIONS

If possible, do this in your parked car or lying on the floor or in bed with really good headphones. It can also be done at a dance party or somewhere with loud music where you feel safe and comfortable enough to lie down and have whatever type of emotional and physical experience you want (i.e., Ecstatic Dance, a place for free-form dance offered in many cities on Sunday mornings and some weekday evenings).

Listen to music that has a strong bass line loud enough so that you actually feel the vibrations. Let it go in through your ears as well as through every skin pore. Feel it in your bones. Feel it filling you up. Penetrating you. Vibrating you. Pleasuring you.

Exercise caution in volume, though; you can even use ear plugs if needed.

Notice when the music builds up toward a climax. There may be multiple instances of this in a song. Let your body relax into them and feel them, making this listening experience *multi-orgasmic* for you.

Start becoming more aware of these sorts of things and delighting in it all. Release shame or judgment about "having a dirty mind" or needing to "get your mind out of the gutter." Instead, give yourself permission to notice and appreciate that life is infused with sexuality. As you do, you'll start to feel sexier by finding the sexy in *all* that's around you.

What You Know ~ Deeper Listening

Now that we've explored the sense of hearing, I want you to explore the practice of a deeper kind of listening: listening to yourself and honing in on your Sixth Sense. The more you fine-tune your ability to listen, to hear, to take in the sounds all around you, the more you can also tune in to hear your inner voice, your inner wisdom, your gut-knowing—the messages coming through your intuition.

Cultivating your intuition can help you know what to eat and how much to eat. This may take some time to develop as a skill, but use the Intuitive Eating practice when you're grocery shopping or trying to figure out what to eat at home.

Practice:

INTUITIVE EATING

This practice will help you start to learn what your body is saying in response to various foods before you even eat them—or decide not to eat them.

- First, begin with your baseline. Close your eyes. Take some breaths. Notice how you feel physically and emotionally.
- Next, open your eyes and pick up a piece of food (or package of food), and notice again how you feel.
- Shut your eyes once more. Take another deep breath, or a few breaths. Do you notice any difference?

You can also try this approach:

- Standing up straight, pick up a piece of food or simply think of a particular food. Notice if you slightly sway forward or backward. Forward indicates a yes. Backward indicates a no. You can practice this by thinking of a food you already know you don't like or is bad for you as well as by thinking of one that you know is good for you and that you do like.

The above practice can be done anywhere. However, it might be easiest at first when you're alone and in a quiet environment. It's within the silence that you can most clearly hear your inner wisdom, your truest and deepest knowings and needs. As you refine this skill, you will be able to hear it even amidst chaos and noise. But first, practice spending time with yourself in silence. This could also be called *meditating*.

Practice:

ENJOYING THE SILENCE
& LISTENING TO YOURSELF

If you don't already have a seated meditation practice, start with as little as five minutes of sitting silently in whatever position is most comfortable for you; you can even lie down if you know you won't fall asleep. Close your eyes. Don't try to force thoughts out of your head, but try not to think. When thoughts arise, just come back to silence and breath.

If your mind is extra noisy, feel free to use a mantra by silently repeating to yourself something like, "Today I intend to listen," or "Here I am," or the Sheng Zhen mantra, "I am a big body of Love. Full of qi, full of Love." Another option is to tell that voice in your head, "Hey, I'm trying to meditate. Let's talk later."

And then spend the next five minutes with your eyes open, notebook open, and pen in hand. Listen, and write whatever wants to come through. This practice can be done for longer, but five minutes sitting and five minutes writing is a great starting point. And who doesn't have ten minutes? Ideally, this is done daily, or twice a day, for maximum benefit and insights.

Use a timer, and consider adding this to your menu and making a contract with yourself.

Advanced Option: Twenty minutes (or more) of meditating followed by twenty minutes (or more) of journaling.

As you cultivate more self-love and deepen your connection with yourself through meditation and other practices within this book, you will be better able to trust what you hear. You will then act more in accordance with your deepest, highest, truest knowing and make more nourishing choices that truly feed you. And that, my friend, is the way to live a multi-orgasmic, amazing life that's in the flow and in alignment. You won't even need to try; you'll just feel better, happier, lighter, brighter. More open to joy and pleasure, and attracting even more joy and pleasure to you like a magnet.

The Art of Sensual Living

Now it's time to put it all together. Isolating the senses just helps you tune into them more. But for optimal benefit, including all of your senses in your dining experiences and sexual experiences—and in all of your life activities—will serve you best in terms of feeling more turned on and fulfilled. I have two practices to help you further awaken your senses and live a more sensual life.

Let's start by taking a little stroll . . .

Practice:

THE MULTI-ORGASMIC WALK

Go for a walk and take in all the smells. Breathe the smell of the dirt and the trees all the way down into your belly. Take in the sights as well. Allow your eyes to be nourished by all of the colors you see, especially the greens. Drink them in.

And notice what you hear around you, whether nature sounds or man-made sounds. Take it all in.

Notice what you feel against your skin, whether your clothing, the breeze, or the warmth of the sun. Reach out and touch some plant life. Can you taste the atmosphere, the environment you're in? Can you taste your own inner environment by moving your tongue around inside of your mouth?

This practice is best done in the woods but can easily be done walking down the street of your neighborhood. Wherever you are, allow your entire body, your entire being, to receive the sensory stimulation that's all around you.

Allow yourself to be penetrated and delighted and filled up with all of this sensory data, again and again and again. Smile, even if it's just an inner smile, as you take it all in. Notice yourself feeling energized and pleasured by all that you see, smell, hear, taste, and feel.

There's something quite magical about being more in touch with your senses and the ways in which that allows you to connect more to nature, to what you eat, to yourself, to others, to all you do and all you are. It's like a reconnecting to that childlike wonder, that sense of enchantment that children have. And now it's time for you to reclaim it, to be enchanted with the trees, with the breeze, the flowers, the bees, and to light up like a little kid with an ice cream cone or watermelon slice regardless of what's on your plate and going into your mouth, even if it's broccoli.

Speaking of what's on your plate, choose at least one meal or snack a day, or even just one a week, to really focus on engaging all of your senses in your dining experience. This practice is designed to engage all of your senses while eating a meal or snacking on a variety of treats. The best way to fully experience this is to listen to the bonus guided recording. But for now, here is a short description of how to experience a Multi-Orgasmic Meal.

It takes time and practice to cultivate your awareness so that you can tap into sensory pleasures all throughout your day and deeply reap the benefits of sensual living. Doing so will help you feel turned on by life. And when you feel turned on, juicy, and alive, you're more likely to make healthier choices and experience fewer unhealthy cravings.

You may notice a huge difference in how you feel the first time you try these above practices, or it may take some patience and persistence. Even if you notice profound shifts right away, the more you explore them on a regular, even *daily*, basis, the more you open up to living consciously, fully aware, and fully embodied. Life will feel richer, and by consciously engaging your senses, you'll also increase your pleasure potential during sex and masturbation, and really in all of your activities. These practices can become a part of how you live your life rather than something you do only until you achieve a specified outcome. The best results come from an ongoing process; whether in the bedroom or the kitchen or the office or the forest, it's about becoming more sensual and living a sensual life.

Practice:

THE MULTI-ORGASMIC MEAL

Arrange for yourself an assortment of finger foods or a meal. For example, you might have strawberries, sugar snap peas, fresh basil leaves, chocolate, almonds, cheese, crackers. The idea is to have a variety of foods with which to experiment. But you can also apply this to a simple meal, such as a bowl of oatmeal or scrambled eggs. This is best done outside but can be done anywhere.

Now, lie or sit down, shut your eyes, and relax your body. Start at your head and work your way down to your toes. The guided audio will take you through a full-body relaxation in which you start to tune in to all of your senses.

- First, notice the feel of the chair or the ground. If you're outside, notice the feel of the breeze or the sun on your skin.

- Next, become aware of what you hear. Planes flying? Your own breath? Birds chirping? And then notice what you smell. Your food? The grass if you're outside?

- Become aware of what you taste, even though you're not eating yet. Move your tongue around inside of your mouth. Can you still taste your previous meal or your toothpaste?

- Next, shift your attention to what you see, keeping your eyes closed. Is it dark? Is it light? Do you see images, colors, or blackness?

- Open your eyes, and again focus on what you see. And then? It's time to eat.

Use your fingers and feel the food. Smell the food. When you take your first bite, shut your eyes again to help you fully taste the food. Repeat this at least several times, if not for the entire meal or snacking experience. Be curious about what you're eating, as if you're eating it for the first time. Look at it, feel it, taste it, smell it. You can even notice the sounds it makes as you chew.

And most importantly? Enjoy!

Please visit www.rebeccacliogould.com/bookbonus *for the full audio recording of this guided exploration.*

START TUNING IN MORE to your senses in your everyday activities. Take some time to **delight in what you feel, see, hear, touch, and taste.** And for an extra dose of sensory yumminess, Lisa Schrader, founder of Awakening Shakti, has contributed her guided Sensual Awakening practice as a book bonus. Lisa is a phenomenal women's empowerment coach who has appeared on *Oprah* and is known for her Shakti Initiation program, among other things. Get a scrumptious little taste of her here: www.rebeccacliogould.com/bookbonus.

Enjoy!

Chapter 8

TAKING MATTERS INTO YOUR OWN HANDS ~ MASTURBATION, SELF-PLEASURING, AND SELF-LOVE

"I believe in the radical power of pleasure, babe."
~ BIKINI KILL

Have you ever seen that old '80s ad from AT&T? The one that told us to "reach out and touch someone"? For a while, I thought this book would have a chapter about sex—with a partner. But here's the deal: I primarily want to empower you to take matters into your own hands and focus on your relationship with yourself. So instead of reaching out and touching someone else, I invite you to reach down and touch yourself.

There are plenty of books out there that can help you with a partner, such as *The Multi-Orgasmic Couple* by Mantak and Maneew Chia, and Douglas and Rachel Carlton Abrams, MD. If you're in a relationship or want to prepare for a sexual partner coming into your life, go out and get that book *after* you work through this one. *The Multi-Orgasmic Diet* is a great first step, a sort of gateway drug into the world of sacred sexuality and Neo-Tantra, which is a modern, western variation of Tantra focused on sex and intimacy practices. And if you want to explore that more at some point, see the Resources section. First things first, though: learning to really, truly love yourself and getting to know your own body and what you like.

Getting to Really Know Yourself

One of my goals here is to help you simply enjoy *life* more. You can do that by taking charge of your life and by taking matters into your own hands—both literally and figuratively. Reaching down and touching yourself—not just with the intent of stimulating your genitals, but touching yourself all over, totally loving yourself up, and getting to know your body—can help you to delight in all of life. Discovering what feels good, what doesn't, what turns you on, and what lights you up can even help you become clearer on your non-sexual desires, likes, and dislikes.

The more you get to know your own body and what you like sexually and sensually, the better you'll know yourself and the more fulfilled and confident you will feel. And I'm going to keep drilling this into your head: **when you feel fulfilled sexually, when you experience pleasure and delight throughout your day, when you feel full of love, and like you're *in Love* regardless of your relationship status, then you are going to see changes in the choices you make around food and activities and even the people in your life.** You're going to eat healthier, and when you *do* give in to a craving, you are going to enjoy it rather than beat yourself up about it.

Furthermore, masturbation, self-pleasuring, and self-love practices are essential parts of learning how to cultivate and harness your sexual energy so that you *have* more energy and feel like a confident, powerful, sexual goddess whose happiness is not dependent on external circumstances or anyone else. No more unconsciously filling a void. You will be fully aware and in total control of your choices, including the choice to consciously relinquish control and indulge in whatever is going to bring you the most joy and satisfaction in any given moment.

When Masturbation is the Answer

I'll tell you the truth: on a plane ride home from Bali in December 2014, I had what felt like a download, a spontaneous creative inspiration—and almost a complete book outline—for *The Multi-Orgasmic Diet.* But I almost ended up calling it "The Masturbation Diet" instead. Shortly after I returned home, I found myself wondering if by masturbating before each meal, or at least once a day, I'd make healthier food choices and my overall well-being would improve. What on earth possessed me to consider this? Why would I think masturbation-induced orgasm could be the answer for everything? *Why on earth wouldn't it be?* Just kidding. Allow me to explain.

I considered that masturbation, with or without orgasm, could be the answer because it's a way to experience pleasure regardless of the other things happening in your life, and it doesn't require a partner. I also considered it as a sort of painkiller during a time when I was feeling lonely and processing a lot of grief. I knew I couldn't attract a healthy partnership coming from a place of such neediness and lack, so I realized I needed to amp up my self-love practices, including masturbation. I needed to feel sexually active and alive even though I was single and not interested in casual sex or in working with a surrogate partner or sexological bodyworker (a sexologist who helps you experience deeper erotic ecstasy and embodiment). And so I decided to partner with myself. I decided to partner with the Divine and with sexual energy itself.

For some time, masturbation *did* feel like the answer. Until I got to a point of "not being in the mood" less than two weeks in. And that's when it became clear to me that what I wanted for myself—and wanted to share with others through this book—was about more than just masturbation and about more than peak orgasm and climax. It's about **feeling the joy of sex with or without sex.** And it's about honoring your natural rhythms and cycles and being true to what it is you really want and need.

Just like there'd be days I might not want to have sex with a partner, there were days I didn't want to have sex with myself. But that didn't mean I didn't want to be held or caressed or gazed at lovingly. So yes, sometimes masturbation is the answer. Sometimes it's a great way to perk yourself up and feel satisfied, sexy, and alive. It can even be used as a manifestation tool! But sometimes you really don't want to masturbate, and that's fine. Don't force it. But do learn more about when and why you may choose to get yourself off.

This practice will help you become more of a conscious lover. It will help you have a deeper understanding of yourself and your sexuality as well as the power of masturbation.

Practice:

CONSCIOUS MASTURBATION

In a notebook or journal, write about your experiences with masturbation. You may choose to consider these questions:

1. When did you first start masturbating? Did you feel good about it, ashamed, embarrassed, or some combination of feelings?

2. How do you feel before you masturbate (emotionally, physically, energetically), and how do you feel after?

3. What usually makes you want to masturbate?

4. Do you use masturbation to numb pain or for the pure pleasure of it?

5. Do you always do the same thing when you masturbate?

6. Do you take your time with it or rush?

There are no right or wrong answers here. This is just about being aware, being conscious of what you're choosing and why.

Benefits of Masturbation

Earlier, I invited you to embrace masturbation as an important part of self-care. Why? In addition to the numerous benefits listed below, your body wants attention and does not like to be ignored. Even if you have a loving and attentive sexual partner—or a sex slave who is available at your beck and call—masturbation is still important. Self-love, self-knowledge, and self-pleasure lead to more confidence, happiness, a radiant glow, better relationships, and better partnered sex.

Masturbation deepens your connection with yourself, helps move your sexual energy, and fills you up with good feelings. It's stress-reducing, as is sex, especially if you let go of agenda. If orgasm is challenging for you, don't worry about cumming; just take time to love yourself up. Be patient with yourself. Explore yourself. Love yourself. And if you still feel pent-up energy, do some sort of cardio or other movement. Get outside. Whack a pillow. Paint. Do whatever it takes to let that energy flow. Reviewing chapter 4 on barriers to orgasm may also be helpful.

The benefits of masturbation include but are not limited to:

- Increases intimacy with self
- Helps you get to know your body
- Promotes a better body image
- Reduces cravings
- Lowers stress
- Relaxes you
- Feels good
- Gets you out of your head and into your body
- Can be meditative, bringing you into the present moment

Reducing Unconscious, Emotional Eating

What I learned from my "masturbation diet" was that it actually *can* be effective for preventing unconscious, emotional eating. For example, for years, I had this habit of eating my parents' chocolate from Trader Joe's every time I would visit them, even though I don't really like it. I don't even eat much chocolate on my own. In fact, I try to avoid sugar and chocolate for the most part because, in addition to the bloating caused by sugar, they both make me anxious after the initial euphoria. Nevertheless, there was always this magnetic pull I'd experience when going back to my childhood home—like functioning on autopilot as

I walked into the kitchen and opened that cabinet. I believe part of it was habit and part of it was some sort of coping mechanism; I'd regress to that fat kid who wanted to self-isolate and just sit on the couch eating sweets.

But when I first had this idea to rename my book "The Masturbation Diet," I started practicing daily self-pleasuring for about ten days. And when I went to visit my parents during the first week of this experiment? I didn't even *think* about that chocolate. For the first time in months, years even, it wasn't a struggle to avoid. I simply made it through the whole day and night without any urge or impulse for chocolate. I didn't even feel tempted to open that cabinet. Why? Because I felt such a deep sense of satisfaction and connection with myself and with this universal, sexual energy that was filling me up. I wasn't yearning for anything unhealthy, and so without even trying, I broke the habit just like that.

Another emotional eating habit I developed in my twenties, oddly enough while studying nutrition, was a nasty habit of devouring a pint of Ben and Jerry's ice cream every week or so during emotionally stressful times—sometimes even more than once a week. It was even my breakfast on law school exam days! And what I've noticed since starting the Multi-Orgasmic Diet myself is that even if I give in to buying that pint, I don't devour the whole thing. And I might not even bother going out to get it after a good self-pleasuring session, or even after a few Orgasmic Breaths or a Multi-Orgasmic Walk around the block.

I'm telling you this because the practices in this book really work. They go deep in creating sustainable changes in how you feel, think, and behave. Instead of focusing on food restrictions and restraint, you focus on experiencing more sexual and sensory pleasure in ways that don't add on the pounds or leave you feeling lethargic, bloated, guilty, or ashamed.

Practice:

THE MASTURBATION DIET

This is simple. All you do is masturbate daily, or every other day, for as long as it seems to be serving you. Daily is best unless you're really not in the mood. And if you are *really* in the mood? More than once a day.

You can masturbate before a meal or when a craving comes on and see how it affects your food choices. Or you can masturbate first thing in the morning to see how starting your day in this way affects you.

Experiment. Be playful with it. Let go of all agenda to cum or quake. Focus on energy, pleasure, joy, letting go.

But how can you let go if you fear being walked in on? If you have children or housemates, perhaps you have some privacy concerns. It can be hard to relax and surrender when afraid of being interrupted. So you may need to get creative with the timing of it or plan in advance. For example, maybe you can't masturbate before a meal or when a craving comes on, but perhaps you can prioritize this activity for times that you know you have the place all to yourself.

If this practice resonates with you, consider adding it to your menu plan and signing a contract. Commit to see results.

Option: As an alternative to the above masturbation practice, you can simply cup your yoni while fully clothed and gently rock your pelvis back and forth to stimulate arousal and sexual energy. Not only is this a good alternative to masturbation, but as sexuality consultant Pamela Madsen teaches in her Lotus Lift Meditation, rocking is also a way to help you get more in touch with your desires and what you truly want.

Note: If you are sexually active with a partner, it's okay to substitute sex for masturbation on your menu plan, sometimes. Just be sure to also take time on a regular basis to be your own lover as well.

Masturbation won't *always* be the answer, at least not for everyone. But you'll never know unless you try. So give it a shot. And if you already masturbate daily, see if you notice any changes by simply having this heightened awareness and setting a specific intention.

Foreplay All Day

Whether you have sex or masturbate daily or not, imagine going through your whole day feeling sexy, alive, and *desired*. Let each moment be an opportunity for arousal, flirtation, and foreplay—with yourself! This will make your day more fun and give you a healthy glow. It will energize you, reduce your cravings, and help you cultivate and harness your sexual energy to use in other endeavors.

Practice:

FONDLING & FLIRTING WITH YOURSELF

Cop a Feel: Cop a feel, with or without looking in the mirror. In the mirror is more fun, more powerful. But if there's not one around, that's fine. Just grab your breast or your butt, or even reach down your panties and feel your warmth, your softness, your wetness. But just a tease. Just for a moment. And then go right back to doing what you were doing. You'll start feeling sexier and more alive. This is especially helpful if there's not someone else in your life who feels you up, flirts with you, and pleasures you.

Wink: Wink at yourself every once in a while. Like when you're washing your hands after going to the bathroom. Or when you catch a glance of your reflection in a window or mirror. Wink at yourself and smile or smirk, thinking, or even saying aloud, *Hey, you sexy thing.*

Have fun with this. If you're at work, go into the bathroom and imagine being ravished by a lover for a quickie. Tousle your own hair, feel yourself up. If you have time, masturbate during your lunch or coffee break and then go right back to work. Why not? Live it up. Be your own lover, whether you have another lover or not.

Foreplay with yourself is also great for when you don't feel in the mood for penetration or orgasm. It also ties into not just going straight to the genitals. There are so many parts of the body that can turn you on and fill you with all sorts of pleasure sensations and joy. It's time to discover, or rediscover, what lights you up when it comes to sensual, nurturing, non-genital touch. The practices in this section—and in this whole chapter—can help you do that.

It's up to you whether you want to focus on loving, nurturing touch that's not necessarily sexually arousing, or if you want to be more of a spunky sex kitten as you play with yourself. I recommend mixing it up, experiencing both. Do what feels best on any given day.

Practice:

HEAVENLY PETTING

Adoringly stroke or pet your head, face, and hair. This can be just a few loving pets or strokes, as if you're washing your face with your hands without water. Or you can go for longer. But it's meant to be super short, most likely less than a minute. It's loving, refreshing, and actually stimulates circulation, resulting in a healthy glow! Visit www.rebeccacliogould.com/bookbonus for my sweet 'n' silly video demonstration.

Falling in Love with Yourself

Speaking of being loving with yourself, one of the most effective self-love practices I know is to look at yourself in the mirror and to learn to love what you see. It's especially important to spend time looking at your reflection in a mirror if you have any body image issues, need to work on self-love, or tend toward feelings of loneliness. You might even need to go out and buy a hand mirror and other mirrors to put up around your home so that you can spend lots of time admiring your own reflection. And don't worry; this doesn't make you a narcissist. This just helps you discover and delight in your own beauty.

Practice:

EYE-GAZING WITH YOURSELF

Get a hand mirror and keep it close to your bed. Start your day by gazing lovingly at your own reflection for a few minutes. If that's too much for you, start with thirty seconds. You can also do this at the end of the day before going to sleep.

See your own beauty, your own sweetness. Give yourself the attention you deserve and crave. Look deeply into your eyes, study your face, make yourself smile. Fall in love with yourself, and everything else will fall into place.

* Add this to your menu and create a contract with yourself. This is one of the most important practices in this book, especially if you're single, but really for everyone.

And if you share your bed with someone but want privacy for the practice, feel free to do it in the bathroom mirror instead.

This eye-gazing practice is powerful when done on a regular basis. And it doesn't need to stop with eye-gazing. Spending time naked and in front of a full-length mirror is an important practice for self-love and self-acceptance; it will help you relax and enjoy yourself and experience more pleasure sexually. The more time you spend naked in front of the mirror *and* touching your body *and* loving yourself, the more likely it is that your food choices will change. You'll befriend your body, and that leads to eating in a way that honors, respects, nourishes, and nurtures this friendship.

Practice:

BEFRIENDING YOUR BODY

Get undressed and stand in front of a full-length mirror. Take yourself in as a whole. Just look at yourself.

It's okay to acknowledge what you don't like, but don't linger there. Cry if you need to cry. And then move on. Look at yourself again, as a whole, and do your best to love yourself as is.

Then, from head to toe, or from toe to head, look at each part of you. Find things you like or love about your body. Thank your various body parts for the many ways in which they serve you. Smile at each part of you. Take in your whole reflection again, and give yourself a hug.

Option: *Use this practice as foreplay with yourself before masturbating, in which case, you might want to light some candles and add in some caresses as you look at your reflection. See yourself as sexy. Let your own reflection turn you on.*

And if you're not feeling turned on, you might want to use some affirmations as you look at your body, such as "I accept you" or "I am learning to love and accept you."

All this mirror work is likely to bring up your inner critic. Maybe even just reading about it does. Remember the inner critic and inner saboteur from chapter 1? It's important to become aware of this inner critic rather than denying it's there or trying to avoid it. Look at yourself and notice what unloving thoughts arise. Acknowledge the self-criticism—let yourself cry and feel the pain too—but then tell your inner critic to shut the fuck up. Review the practices from chapter 1 that address these nasty voices inside, and replace any critical statements with loving, compassionate, kind words to yourself.

Befriending Yoni

There's another part of you that is very important to befriend: the yoni. Remember that yoni is the Sanskrit term for vulva, and it also represents your feminine, creative power. And one of my teachers, Dr. Shakti Malan, likes to think of the yoni as a lotus flower or rosebud with many beautiful layers of petals.

Unfortunately, many women don't think of their yonis as beautiful. Many women have never even fully looked at and explored these various layers. If you never have, you can use a handheld mirror to do so. Or you can go right into the Lotus Flower Breathing practice that was adapted, with permission, from Shakti's book *Sexual Awakening for Women*.

The Lotus Flower Breath will not only help you deepen your connection to yoni, but it can also bring great pleasure and help you cultivate and circulate your sexual energy. I sometimes practice this while driving in my car or instead of a coffee break in the mid-morning or mid-afternoon. It helps me feel more alive, more feminine, sexier, and deeply connected to myself as a multi-orgasmic woman.

Practice:

LOTUS FLOWER BREATHING

Wearing comfortable, loose clothing, sit comfortably in a chair or on a cushion on the floor.

The more gently you can do this practice, the more it will benefit you.

Very gently contract the muscles around the yoni. Think about how when the sun starts to set at night, the lotus flower slowly closes her petals. She has no hurry; she slowly savors the sensation of closing up for the night.

And when the sun rises again, the lotus flower feels the heat and the light of day. Slowly, joyfully, her petals start to unfold and open up to the sun. When the sun is out completely, she is open in her full glory, ready to drink in all that this day brings to her. Her full beauty is seen in her openness and receptivity. Now the bees and the butterflies can come to caress her and play in her nectar.

Let the layers of your yoni open up like that—slowly, curiously, opening to receive the experience of now. Relax completely into the opening. See how deeply you can allow this relaxation and receptivity.

Then the sun sets again, and slowly, the petals of your flower close. Gently contract them. Each time you do this, notice more sensations inside the yoni. Become acquainted with the many petals, as if you can call them each by name. Do the closing very slowly, very gently like that.

Similarly, let the opening be a celebration of sensation. Notice all the subtle sensations through the layers of the yoni as you relax and open up. Also notice new sensations.

Let your pelvis move along in unison. Let your pelvis rock backward and forward along with the opening and closing of the petals. And experiment for yourself with breath. Do you want to breathe in as the petals open and breathe out when the petals close? Or does it feel more natural to breathe out as the petals open and to breathe in when the petals close?

Now let the rest of your body respond along with the opening and closing. Let your inhale open up not only your pelvis but also your breasts, your shoulders, your throat. Allow natural undulations in the body as you open up to the flow of pleasure. Let the breath fall out through an open throat and mouth on the exhale.

Take this rhythm of breathing into a dance of deep delight for yourself—a celebration of your sensuality as a woman.

© 2012 Sexual Awakening for Women by Dr. Shakti Mari Malan, reprinted and adapted with permission.

Beyond the Genitals

It's essential that we pay attention to *all* of the body, both in terms of self-love and in terms of heightening your sexual power. In addition to getting more in touch with yoni and also simply gazing at your body in the mirror and learning to love and accept what you see, it's important to explore and nurture your body with touch.

Practice:

HAND CARESS

One of my favorite ways to self-pleasure and turn myself on is to very lightly caress the back of my hand and fingers with the fingertips of my other hand. The fingertips are sensitive to touch, and the backs of the hands and fingers can be surprisingly responsive to this light touch as well.

You can also use your lips to brush lightly against the backs of your hands. Again, this has potential for double pleasure, as the lips can also feel titillated by the gentle caressing. If partnered, ask your partner to gently lick or bite the backs of your fingers from time to time. It just might make you melt, especially if it's unexpected. You can, of course, also lick and bite yourself, too.

Option: In addition to the hands and fingers, you may also caress the insides of your elbows, forearms, and wrists.

It may feel silly or uncomfortable at first to do something like caress your own hand or lick or bite yourself. But get over it, and get into it. Loosen up. Be curious and playful. Let yourself laugh. And then extend the exploration to your collarbone, shoulders, and breasts.

The breasts may seem like an obvious place for erotic stimulation, but what about for just loving, nurturing touch without the *intent* to arouse? The breasts are far more than erogenous zones for our own pleasure or toys for our lovers. They are also linked to our Hearts, to our ability as women to sustain the life of another, and to our creativity. Loving your breasts and taking good care of them is an act of self-love. My advice to you is to include breast massage as part of your daily wellness routine, along with moisturizing and massaging your entire body.

Practice:

FULL-BODY BREAST MASSAGE

Maybe you've always been good about moisturizing your face and even your legs and arms. But what about your entire body, from head to toe? What about your breasts and your nipples specifically?

Moisturize your whole body using your favorite oil or moisturizer, and don't leave out the breasts. Take this time to lovingly touch and moisturize every part of you, and give some extra attention to your breasts by actually massaging them.

Option: This also can be an opportunity to experiment with various types of touch. You can play around with a firm or light touch, stroking or scratching, pressing, etcetera. Discover more about what types of touch you like and dislike.

Moisturizing and massaging your entire body, every day, while thinking about it as an act of love and nurturing, is a great way to cultivate a healthier relationship with it. It's a wonderful way to start off the day by feeling loved, touched, and cared for by somebody, and delighting in knowing that somebody is you. And that somebody is always going to be there and can give you the love and attention you desire and deserve.

Using Your Voice

When you masturbate or self-pleasure in other ways, say *yes*. Yes to what you're doing, and "yes" out loud. *Yes, yes, yes!* Affirm your pleasure. Affirm that you deserve it. But not silently. Use your voice. Why? Because it's sexy. Feeling confident and open and free to express yourself and use your voice is incredibly sexy.

If you're not partnered, it can be fun to talk to yourself when you're being your own lover, or even to occasionally just blurt out "yes, Yes, *Yes! Oh, God, Yes!*" for a little pick-me-up and to make yourself smile and laugh, maybe even blush. Plus, as mentioned in chapter 3, it will also help you feel more comfortable and natural in saying it when with someone. So if you're not partnered, or if you are but feel shy, just practice on your own. Practice gets you accustomed to something and helps you move through your blockages to learn and grow. Plus, loosening the flow of energy through your throat just might help loosen you up sexually; vocal cords and vaginal tissue are the same kind of tissue! So relax and open your throat to help relax and open your yoni. Be vocal. Grunt, groan, moan.

Making Love to Yourself

It's time to put everything you've read so far into effect. Schedule a date with yourself. Give yourself plenty of time. You can take yourself out first or go straight to the bedroom. Treat yourself as you'd wish to be treated by your ideal dream lover, whether you have a real one or not. Get romantic with yourself. Get sexy with yourself. Fall totally in love and into a sea of ecstasy with yourself. The following practice has various parts. If you can take time for all of them, fantastic! If not, modify as needed.

Practice:

A NIGHT OF SENSUAL SELF-PLEASURING

Part 1: Start by feeding yourself, whether it's a whole meal or a small snack. Use the Multi-Orgasmic Meal guided audio, or simply remember to shut your eyes and savor the flavors.

Part 2: If you have a bathtub, give yourself a bath. A bubble bath is ideal. Delight in the bubbles, feeling them against your skin. Touch yourself anywhere and everywhere you want. Rinse off with the shower, and feel as if your body is being kissed by each drop of water. Thousands of kisses raining down on you. Do this all by candlelight if possible, with or without music playing; remember, you can hear a symphony in anything.

Part 3: Dry yourself off, lovingly. Massage your skin, every inch of you, with coconut oil or your favorite moisturizer, slowly, luxuriating in it. Take this time to explore your own landscape, discovering all of your unmapped erogenous zones. **Option:** You can spray yourself with rosewater first and/or add essential oil to your moisturizer if you want.

Part 4: Stand in front of a full-length mirror in a candlelit or dimly lit room, still naked, or slowly disrobe or remove your towel as you watch your reflection. Start by looking at your whole self, and then focus in on your eyes. Gaze into your eyes and then study your face, seeing your beauty. And then continue moving your gaze down and around, taking in each and every part of your body. You can touch yourself while looking at yourself, or you can just look. Look yourself up and down like a lover. Let yourself feel turned on by what you see.

Part 5: Get into bed. Touch yourself all over, gently, lovingly, seductively, playfully. Use your mouth, too. Kiss yourself or run your lips over your skin. Give yourself little love bites, perhaps on your fingers or wrists. Play with your hair. Pull on it if you like.

Part 6: Enter the temple, but first just rest; place one hand over your yoni, another hand on your heart or a breast. Keep your hand on your yoni until she welcomes you in. Peak orgasm is welcome but isn't the goal here. Just feel what you feel. No agenda. Just presence and pleasure.

Yum! I'm feeling pretty speechless after that. How about you? Are you getting out your calendar yet to schedule it in? Or does it feel like too much for you?

Remember, you are in total control here. You can spend as much or as little time as you want being your own lover. And self-pleasuring can occur with or without peak orgasm and with or without penetration. You might even feel orgasmic pleasure pulsing through you while simply reading that or while sitting to meditate! Just follow your feeling. Do whatever feels best and is going to bring you the most pleasure as you explore how masturbation, self-pleasuring, and self-love can feed you.

BE PATIENT AND GENTLE with yourself as you incorporate these practices into your life and cultivate a deeper level of intimacy with *you*. And have fun with this! If you have already started using a meal plan template, now is a great time to add to it.

Chapter 9

CRAVINGS, CURIOSITY, AND CREATIVITY

*"Cravings are not about food.
Cravings are about stress."*

~ MELISSA HARTWIG

Let's face it. Oftentimes we crave things that aren't so good for us. But that can change, both in terms of developing healthier cravings and in terms of feeling good about *anything* we crave. The truth is that crappy food and binge eating numb us and keep our energy suppressed and blocked. It's a vicious cycle because trapped energy creates anxiety and depression, and that can trigger unhealthy eating patterns. However, the cravings and impulses for crappy food and binging are trying to tell us something. This chapter is about how to use cravings to your advantage by listening to them. It's about getting curious and creative when they strike and also indulging in maximum pleasure when you do give in.

On that note, be forewarned that **this chapter may actually *cause* cravings.** I can't tell you how many times I found myself craving pizza or ice cream while working on this book, especially this chapter and chapter 11! But guess what I did? Sometimes I gave in and enjoyed the heck out of it, consciously delighting in each bite. But most of the time, I'd go for a walk, take some Orgasmic Breaths, or enjoy a self-pleasuring break instead, and I always felt more energized and at peace afterward. So if you notice your own cravings getting stirred up in this chapter or anywhere else in this book, you can turn to your menu. Or simply acknowledge them in the practices that follow, and you may learn what your body really wants instead of food.

Cravings as Messengers

Sometimes a craving is a straightforward, crystal clear desire for the actual thing your body is asking for. But sometimes there's something else you need, or at least something else that can satisfy you. And that *something else* can take the form of nutrients, actions, or emotions.

For example, craving chocolate could indicate that your body needs more magnesium. Or it could be that you're craving physical touch, a feeling of satisfaction through the pleasure of connection, or a rush of oxytocin. It could mean that you're thirsty or that you're feeling sad and could use a hug or a walk in some fresh air. Craving a snack, in general, could indicate that your blood sugar is low and you really do need some food. But often, cravings are born out of thirst, boredom, depression, anxiety, or even habit.

So get curious. Not suspicious, shameful, or restrictive. Just curious.

Practice:

IDENTIFYING DEEPER CRAVINGS

At the first sign of a craving, shut your eyes and take a deep breath. Ask yourself:

- Am I thirsty?
- Am I sleepy?

- How am I feeling emotionally?
- How do I want to feel?
- What do I really want?

Maybe you just need some water. Or maybe you really want to snuggle or laugh with a lover or friend instead of eating half a pizza or drinking that glass of wine. Or maybe you really do want that pizza or wine, but it's unlikely you'll consume as much of it if you're being mindful of your deeper feelings, desires, and needs. You can even enjoy it more now, guilt-free.

As you become more conscious of what underlies your cravings, you'll be empowered to choose whether or not, and *how*, to act on them. When you get curious, you'll find the healthiest ways to satisfy your cravings and gain more clarity about what it is you truly want or need.

Identifying Needs and Addressing Neediness

Speaking of needs, it's okay to have them. In fact, it's healthy to acknowledge our needs and find ways to get them met. Usually we think of food, water, and shelter as basic, non-negotiable needs. Yet we may deny ourselves sufficient amounts of love, touch, and sexual gratification. The anxiety associated with not receiving enough love, touch, and sexual gratification can result in overeating to fill a void or excessive sugar cravings to make up for a lack of sweetness in one's life. Denying these needs, or having them denied by others, may also show up as a form of masochism and self-restriction in which one doesn't eat enough or cannot delight in the eating experience.

Why is this such a challenge for women in particular? Because women receive messages about how we *shouldn't* be needy. The thing is, we all have needs. So what's the difference between needs and neediness? Neediness comes through when we deny our needs and are feeling incomplete. To prevent unhealthy eating habits and a shame-ridden mentality, we must learn to identify and voice our needs. Doing so will also enhance our pleasure potential and quality of life.

Becoming aware of your needs, and accepting them, will actually help you feel *less* needy. Rather you'll feel empowered to make sure that your needs are being met in the healthiest, most fulfilling of ways. And when you are fulfilled, you will feel happier, crave more of what serves you well, and exude a sexy, radiant glow!

Practice:

ASSESSING YOUR NEEDS

Step 1: Make a list of your needs. Don't censor yourself. Later you can see if some of these things aren't necessary. And don't get too philosophical about it, such as by thinking, *Well, I only really need food, water, shelter, etcetera.* Be as flamboyant as you want. Need a new car? Need to win the lottery? Great! Write it down.

Step 2: Circle the things that are absolute, basic, must-have needs. List where and how you get these needs met.

Step 3: For the needs that weren't circled, like "winning the lottery," write out why you need that. What will it do for you? How will it make you feel? You may want to refer back to chapter 1 for Laura Lavigne's concept of Essence vs. Form. And then? See where else you can meet these needs.

Junk Food vs. Comfort Food

Now, before we dive more deeply into this chapter, I want to clarify something. You may have noticed I used the terms "junk food" or "junky food" and "comfort food" earlier in the book. I don't know about you, but I grew up hearing the term "junk food" left and right. Partially because I was eating a lot of it, and partially because my parents were big dieters and that was a popular term in the '80s. So for most of my life, I would eat a lot of candy, ice cream, and baked goods, thinking of it all as "junk food." Calling it "junk" didn't stop me from wanting it or eating it. But it did stop me from feeling good—about myself, my body, and my food choices.

What kind of message is it to be feeding yourself with "garbage" or something you think of as "bad" for you? Masaru Emoto, author of *The Hidden Messages of Water*, has found that water is affected by words. And since we are composed of over sixty percent water, our bodies are affected by the words we use, whether we speak them out loud or silently say them to ourselves.

There's no denying that words have power. So if you're eating something that you think of as *junk, garbage, crap, bad for you, going to make you sick, going to make you fat*, well, what do you think is going to happen? A self-fulfilling prophecy. And even if you do enjoy the indulgence to some extent, it's unlikely you'll be able to tap into your *full* pleasure potential because of underlying feelings of guilt, shame, or fear.

Sometimes I even wonder if watching what you think is more important than watching what you eat. And I certainly believe that cleaning up your thoughts can help clean up your diet. When your thoughts are positive and in alignment with your greatest good, then what you eat will be good for you, too, even if you choose to indulge in sugary sweets and fried or cheesy yumminess from time to time.

Practice:

WATCH WHAT YOU THINK

If you're going to eat ice cream, pizza, French fries, and whatever other "junk" foods float your boat, watch your language. *Please* think of what you're eating as *comfort* food rather than junk food. This will help you more fully enjoy and delight in it. Rather than giving your body the message that you're feeding it junk, you'll be giving your body the message that you're loving it the best you can with this "comfort" food. Make sense?

Notice if with the above practice your bullshit meter—that part of you that doesn't yet believe your positive thoughts—goes off on alert. If it does, you can use this mantra: *"I intend for this food to be a comforting treat and a pleasure to eat."* Chances are you'll eat less of the thing and enjoy it a heck of a lot more than before.

Now, let's look at some of the most common types of food cravings and compulsions: sugar, salt, fat, and chocolate.

Sugar

Sugar, *mmm*, sweet sugar. Sugar cravings usually indicate you are deficient in certain nutrients (i.e., chromium), need more water, or need more sweetness in your life. However, it could also be an indication of parasites or candida. Because they feed off of sugar, you are likely to experience an increase in cravings if you have an infestation or overgrowth. Sometimes it's even excessive sugar cravings that can alert you to one of these two things wreaking havoc in your system. But that is beyond the scope of this book.

So parasites and candida aside, the first thing I recommend you do when sugar cravings strike? Simply drink some water. Also consider eating something like a carrot or an apple instead of something with refined sugar. And before putting any food into your mouth, give yourself some love and sweetness, such as with one of the previous self-love practices in this book or the Be Sweet to Yourself practice. Making sure you have enough sweetness in your life is likely to diminish your sweet tooth.

Practice:

BE SWEET TO YOURSELF

When you feel a strong urge to eat sweets, take some time to be sweet to yourself. First, notice your craving. Next, shut your eyes, take a deep breath, and acknowledge that you're needing some sweetness. Consider placing a hand on your heart with or without your other hand on your belly. You can then be sweet to yourself through touch, words, and/or looking at your reflection in a mirror.

Another option is to do something sweet for yourself, like buying yourself some flowers, writing a love letter to yourself, or taking yourself out on a date. This is also an opportunity for a self-pleasuring session. If you need a quick fix, and orgasm is easy for you, go ahead and get yourself off with the intention of it being something sweet you're doing for yourself.

If you have time for a longer self-lovemaking session, go all out. You may wish to use the Sensual Self-Pleasuring practice in chapter 8. Get some candles, play some sexy music, tell yourself all the sweet things you want to hear, and touch yourself all over. Fill up on your own sweetness, relaxing and opening so that your sexual energy can flow and fill you up even more.

While it's important for you to be able to self-soothe and self-love, there's no denying that human connection and interaction with others is a basic need and important to your well-being. So don't be shy. Be brave. It's okay for your act of self-love to be reaching out to someone else.

Practice:

ASK FOR SOME SWEETNESS

Call or text a friend, and be honest about how you feel. You can say something like "Hey, I'm noticing I'm feeling a need for some sweetness. Are you available for a hug and some snuggling? Or going to a silly movie? Or can you tell me what you like about me over the phone?" If you've never done anything like this before, or the person you're calling is new to this type of request, it can be helpful to provide options. Otherwise, sometimes all you must say is that you're needing some sweetness, and then see what he or she has to offer.

The more you love yourself up and delight in self-induced pleasure on a regular basis, and the more comfortable you become with reaching out to others, the less likely you'll be to crave and reach for unhealthy snacks or *over*indulge when you do decide to indulge. Why? Because you'll feel satisfied and full of sweetness and Love.

Now, if drinking water, or loving yourself up, or letting someone else shower you with kindness still doesn't do the trick? It could be that you just really want that sugary treat, and that's okay. Or it could mean that sweet foods are actually missing from your diet. But that doesn't mean you need to eat refined sugar. You can eat fruits and vegetables like carrots or sugar snap peas. Also, the more you chew grains and starchy vegetables, the sweeter they become while still in your mouth.

Practice:

CHEW YOUR WAY TO SWEETNESS

Cook some brown rice or lightly steam some carrots. It's also okay to use raw carrots for this practice. Aim for chewing thirty times. Yes, thirty times. Depending on how much rice or carrot you put in your mouth, thirty might be too much, but you get the point. Chew, chew, and chew some more. Liquefy the food in your mouth. In addition to bringing out the sweetness, this is good for digestion as well as developing more mindfulness while eating. You're also likely to eat less because you'll be eating more slowly, giving yourself time to feel satisfied.

With the rice, if it's still not sweet enough for you, add some *raw* carob powder with or without stevia. You may also add shredded beets and/or carrots.

As mentioned above, you can use natural sugar alternatives, such as stevia, which is a naturally sweet, green leafy plant. It is known to *not* affect blood sugar levels, *not* cause inflammation, and *not* feed candida or parasites. It can satisfy your sweet tooth without contributing to weight gain or triggering more cravings. Just be very careful with dosage. If you use too much, it can be hard to shake the aftertaste. I recommend *whole* stevia, which is the brown liquid or green powder, rather than the more commonly used clear liquid or white powder. Xylitol also may be a good sugar alternative for you, but when used in excess, *some* report gas, bloating, or loose stools. So go easy on it when first experimenting.

Salt

All that talk about sugar is making me think about salt now. Do you ever crave salt after a sugar binge? I know I do. And it makes sense. Why? Because sugar depletes minerals, and salt cravings tend to indicate a lack of trace minerals. These trace minerals can be found in salt. But even if you eat salt, you might not be getting these minerals because common table salt is stripped of them. Table salt also contributes to bloating. Using Celtic sea salt or Himalayan pink salt will give you the minerals you need, and they're less likely to lead to bloating. Pumpkin seeds, cacao, and sea veggies will also boost your mineral intake and, therefore, prevent these cravings.

Another solution is mineral supplements. Sometimes I recommend using a supplement during a transitional phase, while you're learning how to get more of the nutrients you need from whole foods. Remember, it's all about experimenting and making long-term, sustainable changes. Don't just buy a supplement thinking it's a quick fix. And don't think a supplement is a waste of money and write off the possibility of it helping. Give it some time, like a month or two, and pay attention to what, if anything, changes. On the other hand, sometimes people notice a dramatic improvement within the first day or week of taking a new supplement. For instance, once upon a time, I'd been feeling down in the dumps for a week or so, and on the first day of adding in a vitamin D3 supplement, I suddenly noticed I felt high as a kite and couldn't stop smiling! While I'm not certain it was the D3 or just a really good day, I have found supplements can really help on occasion.

Fat

Guess what? Fat is essential for the healthy functioning of your body and your brain, including your libido and orgasmic potency. You *do* need to consume some fat. The question is what type and how much. Eating jalapeño poppers and French fries might satisfy your cravings and taste buds, but they're actually giving you the kind of fat that you *don't* want. Experiment with eating healthier fats, such as avocados, raw nuts, nut butter, olives—even jalapeño stuffed olives. You can include these foods in your diet, and then see if your cravings diminish.

Healing your relationship with fat may also be necessary. If you're currently, or ever have been, overweight, then the word "fat" can sound like a dirty word—an insult, something to avoid at all costs, and something to keep hidden from others. There's that shame again. Also, sometimes craving extra fat and putting on the pounds can be a form of protection from unwanted sexual attention. So if you have any excess fat on your body, let's do a little practice to release shame and hatred and to instead love and appreciate fat for its vital role in our lives.

Practice:

BEFRIENDING FAT

If you have a little, or a lot, of extra fat on you, I invite you to befriend it. With or without looking in the mirror, touch your body where you have some extra cushioning, and view it as that: a cushion. View it as luscious, soft, and sensual rather than something to loathe, curse, or get rid of.

Talk to it. If it's there as protection, thank it for protecting you. Have a conversation—silently or out loud—about how you're ready to feel safe as a sexual being in the world now and don't need this extra fat hiding you and protecting you from harm.

Thank it for protecting you, whether physically, emotionally, or energetically. Remind it of its importance and role in your health. Then explain that you're ready to release some of it now.

Chocolate

Chocolate. *Mmmmm.* What more is there to say?

Don't worry—I'm not going to tell you to stop eating chocolate. Instead, I'll share a story and a practice with you that will help you derive even more pleasure from this commonly craved treat while *effortlessly* eating less of it.

It started like this: one morning, I was craving some chocolate and remembered I had a stevia-sweetened chocolate bar in my pantry. As I broke off just one little rectangle, I remembered receiving an offering in a women's group the previous day that just happened to be chocolate as well. We were exploring our inner goddess and our divinity, and while I reflected on those offerings, I put the tiny morsel in my mouth, let it slowly dissolve, savoring it, and thought of myself as a goddess. The result? I spontaneously committed to eating only one rectangle per day, maybe two. I also vowed to let each piece of chocolate slowly dissolve rather than devouring the whole bar within a couple of days. Why? Because in addition to cutting down on the amount of chocolate I'd consume, it also *felt* so much more loving, honoring, and delightful to pleasurably suck than to compulsively chew.

Practice:

CHOCOLATE OFFERING TO THE GODDESS

If chocolate is one of your temptations, and you're likely to eat a lot of it at once, try this: get a chocolate bar, your favorite kind, or one of the stevia-sweetened bars if you're cutting out sugar.

At first, don't restrict yourself by saying you'll only eat one square/rectangle. Instead, simply commit to letting the chocolate melt in your mouth. Really take your time. Savor it. Don't multitask. Make a ritual of it. Delight in it. Breathe deeply. Shut your eyes. Enjoy it.

And then see if you even want more, or if you're feeling satisfied already.

This practice resulted in these words going through my head: "Feed yourself as if you're making an offering to the goddess." And then it occurred to me to let *everything* I take into my body be an offering. Whether it's chocolate, pizza, water, or wine in your mouth, whether it's coconut oil or moisturizer on your skin, or a penis, finger, or dildo in your yoni, let it all be an offering to the goddess that you are.

Satisfying Oral Fixations with Mouthwatering Mouthgasms

One primary way in which we derive pleasure is through the mouth, and there's nothing wrong with having a craving for something, *anything*, to be in your mouth. Oral fixations start for us as babies, as it's how we receive nourishment and nutrients as well as comfort and a sense of safety in terms of survival. That's partially why food and dieting can be such a touchy subject and challenge for some folks; it's wrapped up in what we know of survival, comfort, and love.

There's also a sexual component to consider here: oral sex, or even just some PG-13 French kissing. If you feel a craving for either of these but don't have a partner, or your partner isn't around, there are other options. For instance, chia seed pudding has been known to satisfy my sexual oral desire and prevent me from overindulging in ice cream. There's something about the way it feels in my mouth and on my tongue and going down my throat—that sensual quality does the trick. It's so yummy in terms of the experience, texturally and sensually. Plus, there are various ways to flavor the pudding and play with the consistency to make it work for you. Or you can buy it ready-made; see the Shopping List in Appendix 2. Either way, you can use the following practice to experiment with the pleasure of sensual eating.

Practice:

MULTIPLE MOUTHGASMS

Get some chia seed pudding. Or you can use a banana (mashed up or whole), a mango, or anything else that would be fun to lick, suck, or slurp. You can even use ice cream, and this practice can help you derive more pleasure from it, and therefore, most likely, eat less of it. Here's what you do:

Put the treat of your choice into your mouth. Shut your eyes. Breathe. Play around with the food in your mouth, using your tongue. Hone in on the taste and the texture. Breathe the pleasure of it down to your Heart, through your breasts, and all the way into your yoni. Swallow slowly, and lick your lips in satisfaction after each mouthful.

The previous practice for eating chocolate is one of my favorite ways to experience a mouthgasm. And, honestly, you can mouthgasm with anything. Perhaps you already experienced this when you played with your food or ate with your eyes closed in chapter 7.

Exploring the Connection between Happiness and Food

Sometimes you can even experience a mouthgasm without food in your mouth, just like you can have a wet dream. While in the midst of writing this book, I heard something on the radio about how there are certain foods that make people happy simply by *thinking* about them. My ears immediately perked up. Can you guess what those foods are?

Number one was ice cream. And number two was chocolate. I don't know what the third one was, but it doesn't really matter what other people experience. What matters is what *you* experience. What foods make *you* happy just by thinking of them? Do you ever stop yourself from feeling happy because you're ashamed and feel like you shouldn't want or delight in those foods?

I invite you now to let food make you happy, to **shamelessly welcome food as a source of pleasure.** Start with a list.

Practice:

HAPPY FOODS

Which foods make you happy?

Which foods make you happy just by simply thinking about them?

As you go throughout your day, your week, your month, and beyond, take note of foods that make you happy. They might not all come to you now. Plus, as you continue with the practices in this book, over time, your preferences and what makes you happy just might change (i.e., sugar snap peas or chia seed pudding instead of ice cream!).

This idea of a food bringing happiness simply by thinking about it highlights the power of the mind in terms of cravings and how we handle them. Consider, for example, that eating ice cream may be delightful because of the feel of it in your mouth, but what you really want is oral sex or a hot 'n' heavy make-out session. Or maybe you just want love and affection and sweetness from your sweetheart. But if you don't have a sweetheart, or that person is not available, instead of eating ice cream, you could go masturbate, kiss your hand, or feel yourself up. You could just breathe. You can even think about the food you're craving *while* pleasuring yourself! No judgment.

And no fear. It's okay to feel nervous or uncomfortable, but we don't want to let it get in our way. Fear robs us of our happiness. Unfortunately, it's often used as a way to get people to stop eating what's bad for them. I'm not a doctor, and I don't know what your state of health or disease is (unless we're working together in a coaching program), but there are some scenarios which really require you to be strict about cutting something out of your diet. But let's say that's not the case here. Then why demonize food?

Although scare tactics may be necessary for some, I don't recommend using fear or negative associations as a diet method. For example, instead of equating white sugar with rat poison or with getting fat or having diabetes, consider the idea of letting sugar be something that makes you happy *but not something you have to ingest to feel that way.* Remember? Certain foods can make us feel good just by thinking of them. There are also many healthy alternatives.

This concept can extend into other parts of your life as well. For example, let's say you're in a relationship. The thought of your partner can make you happy without him or her even being present. Just let yourself feel the joy and pleasure that thoughts of that person bring regardless of whether you come into contact with him or her. This applies to food and objects as well. It doesn't matter if it's good or bad for you, just let yourself feel the desire, the arousal, and the happiness associated with those people, foods, or objects.

By doing this, you learn to delight in the fantasy while still being grounded in reality. Your mind is a powerful thing, so use it to your advantage to make yourself feel good. It's from that place of fulfillment that you will effortlessly attract and choose more goodness.

The Importance of Creativity and Having Creative Outlets

Our culture is full of excess consumption. *Shop, shop, shop. Buy, buy, buy. Bigger is better. Eat more and more.* And if you're not consciously creating on a regular basis, you're more likely to be part of this consumption machine. How so? You just might attempt to fill your mouth and belly instead of attaining fulfillment through creative expression and contribution.

Motivational speaker Tony Robbins says that contribution is actually one of our six human needs. And I've heard Reverend Dr. Kathianne Lewis, of Seattle's Center for Spiritual Living, speak of an increased compulsion to consume when not creating. I would add that part of that, whether conscious or not, is because of the anxiety you experience when you're not living up to your highest purpose or fully expressing yourself and your creative potential.

You are here because of an act of creation, and **you are an inherently creative being, whether you realize it or not.** It's important to feed this part of yourself, not only with food, but through the act of creative expression—whether it's cooking a meal, drawing or painting, designing a website, writing, getting dressed up, assembling a piece of furniture, or even daydreaming. There are so many ways to create and be creative.

This goes for men, too. But women, in particular, were made to create. Our wombs contain this creative, generative, sexual power. Even if you no longer have a uterus, the energetic imprint and power of your uterus is still there. Regardless of *procreation*, *creation* is your super power. So let it flow. Express it. Give birth to something.

Practice:

GET CREATIVE

If you have blank paper and markers or crayons, get them out. If not, use any paper and a pen or pencil, or save this practice until after you've gone to the store.

1. Sit comfortably. Shut your eyes (after reading this). Breathe. Notice your breath. Feel your body softening and relaxing.

2. Bring your attention into your head, into your mind. Then drop your attention down into your Heart, and then even further down into your womb, and into your yoni.

3. Ask yourself, "What do I want to create? What wants to be birthed through me?" You may also ask these questions in each location: head, Heart, womb, and yoni.

4. Continue breathing and softening your body. Listen to what answers come. See what visuals arise.

5. And when you're ready, open your eyes and start writing or drawing.

I encourage you to use color. Even if you don't feel artistic or don't know how to draw, simply using colored markers or crayons will help you tap into your creativity. Even if all you write is "I don't know," make that statement colorful or doodle around it. Fill the page.

Tip: Watercolors are also a wonderful way to quickly and easily take a creativity break in your day. You don't need to paint anything specific. You can simply fill the paper with colors as a meditation or a form of color therapy.

Option: In addition to coloring books becoming a popular form of meditation for adults, using coloring books can also help you tap in to your creativity. For an extra boost of self-love and body-positive messages along with your coloring, I highly recommend *The Love Yo'Self Coloring Book* by Sara Young.

How'd you do? Are you feeling blocked creatively? Sex and masturbation can help. Not only does it help you relax, but it stimulates your sexual energy, which is also your creative energy. A lot of this book was inspired in moments of living my own multi-orgasmic life. There was one day in particular when I kept interrupting myself during a self-pleasuring session to jot down ideas that were coming to me about this book! See? One thing led to another. And the actual act of sex or masturbation isn't even a necessity; simply tapping into your sexual energy can help unblock you. By learning to channel your sexual (and creative) energy, you will feel sexier and happier, more alive, and more fulfilled. Remember that the Sex Energy Circulation practice from chapter 2 might be helpful here as well.

Getting Curious about Creative Alternatives

Now that you're more aware of various factors that play into your cravings, it's time to go beyond the Deeper Cravings practice from the beginning of this chapter. It's time to clearly identify why you crave what you crave and get curious and creative about alternatives that can help you feel better.

As cliché as it may sound, awareness truly is the first step. Be patient with yourself when implementing changes. Having a list of alternatives taped to your fridge or somewhere handy will serve you well. And remember, if you do give in to the initial craving, enjoy the heck out of it! Really get into the pleasure of it. And over time, you'll find that you give in less and less as you opt for other ways of filling yourself up and feeling delight.

Practice:

TRIGGERS, CRAVINGS, & ALTERNATIVES

Part 1: Take a moment now to think about your most common cravings. List them, and then list alternatives. If you're aware of what triggers the craving, include that as well. You can also use this in the moment that a craving arises.

Trigger (optional)	Food/ Behavior	Alternatives/Solutions
i.e., seeing my ex	ice cream	chia seed pudding, paint, cry, hit a pillow, dance
i.e., no evening plans	late-night snacking	sleep, take a bath, drink tea, call a friend

Part 2: Write or type out a list of the alternatives, whether alternative foods or alternative activities. Put this list on your fridge, type it up in your smartphone, or keep it in your purse—wherever it's most likely to help you when a craving comes on.

The Importance of Mindfulness and Setting Intentions

You'll start taking a healthier approach to all of life simply by setting your intentions, identifying your needs, and being more consciously aware and mindful. For example, let's say you decide that a pint of ice cream *is* the best choice for meeting your needs in a given moment. At least now you're doing it consciously, and hopefully *without* shame. What I've found is that even if I buy the pint and give myself permission to devour it, it takes much less to satisfy me because I'm already feeling good about my choice to indulge.

As mindful eating expert Geneen Roth shares, sometimes we do things that are bad for us *because* we're punishing ourselves and/or actually want to be bad. If you give yourself permission and take the guilt, shame, and taboo out, you will discover a new sense of freedom to enjoy this behavior. Alternatively, it may no longer feel as delightful or tempting. For example, the first half cup or so of ice cream might be really delicious and feel good, but then you'll notice that it's not as much fun to keep going. You'll fill up on the pleasure of it *and* on treating yourself well. The void you were trying to fill will be partially filled with ice cream and partially filled with self-love and delight. This is a gradual, gentle, and loving approach to cutting down on binges and unhealthy eating patterns.

Final Thoughts on Cravings

It's okay to crave what you crave, and, assuming no serious health issues, it's okay to give in sometimes to things we might consider "bad for us." You don't have to always find a substitution. But you do need to stop thinking of it as "bad" if you're going to eat it.

When you feel bad about what you've eaten, it defeats the whole purpose of trying to feel good and experience more pleasure. Plus, negative thoughts about what you eat can result in creating a dis-ease process in your body. So be careful what you think—not fearful, just careful and mindful. Think good, loving, nurturing thoughts about what you take into your body, regardless of what it is.

And if you're going to indulge in a craving for something like ice cream or pizza, or reach out to a partner for sex, let it be from a place of already feeling filled up and content rather than down or empty. It's natural, and can even be *healthy*, to give in to your food cravings or reach out for connection, but let's try to go about it from a place of already feeling good.

That being said, you don't need to feel great in order to reach out to somebody. One benefit of friendships and relationships is receiving support and an energy boost from your interaction. After all, we all need people. But the idea here is that it's important to do your practices and take good care of yourself so you can remember that the core of your being contains your own essence, bliss, and contentment. So reach out consciously rather than in an unconscious sort of default mode. It's okay to need others, social interaction, and even food, to increase your energy and alter your mood, but be aware of what you're doing, and do your part to feel your best on your own.

THIS WEEK, COMMIT TO raising your awareness regarding your cravings. Start playing around with healthy substitutions as well as taking some time for creativity. When you do give in to a craving, let yourself truly enjoy it, taking the pleasure into each and every cell of your being!

Chapter 10

MOVE IT OR LOSE IT

*"Movement should be approached like life—
with enthusiasm, joy, and gratitude—
for movement is life, and life is movement,
and we get out of it what we put into it."*

~ RON FLETCHER

Movement is a crucial part of living a healthy life and enjoying it to the fullest. But many people view movement, in the form of exercise, as a chore. I used to think of it that way as well, plus I believed it was something I *should* do to improve myself. Over the past twenty-something years, I've tried using a stationary bike, cross-country skiing machine, and an elliptical. I also gave personal training, running, and a whole slew of workout videos and DVDs a whirl. But it wasn't until I used Insanity®, a series of high-intensity interval training workout DVDs put out by Beach Body®, that I realized the benefit was really more about making me feel good than changing my looks.

Before that epiphany, my primary motivation was insecurity—I felt self-conscious and wanted to look better, feel sexier, and be more attractive. I believed that meant having a body that looked a certain way. What I've delightfully discovered since then is that sex appeal radiates from the inside out. Some of the sexiest women I know would be considered "out of shape," and yet they exude a confidence, sensuousness, and sex appeal like no others.

If what you look like, or want to look like, feels like an effective and healthy form of motivation, fine. But **I encourage you to focus more on what the exercise is doing for you deep within.** Is it strengthening your muscles, giving you pleasure, or making you happy? How's it affecting your endurance, your mood, and your confidence?

Imagine exercise being something you actually look forward to and slimming down or getting healthier as being fun and freeing. Imagine living a more pleasurable life—an active life—and burning more calories doing things that feel natural instead of being forced. Imagine being so busy enjoying your day that you don't even think (as much) about needing to diet because it just isn't a priority and no longer feels like a job. This is really possible! As you incorporate the Multi-Orgasmic Diet into your life, you may find yourself *wanting* to work out and move more. You might naturally start to gravitate toward activities that burn calories and possibly also build strength and flexibility. And you'll probably enjoy it!

Use your body while you've got it, which is what "move it or lose it" really means. It also refers to the mental and emotional benefits of incorporating plenty of physical movement into your life. Tension and frustration can build, depression can deepen, and anxiety can increase when you're too sedentary. Physical movement facilitates the release and transformation of these emotions so that you don't lose your cool. So, in whatever capacity you can, work it. Be your best, but not by society's standards or media images. Be your *own* best, whatever that is for you.

Revamping a Sedentary Lifestyle

Considering all of the physical and emotional health benefits of movement, it may come as no surprise to you that one of the most common reasons for health problems is a sedentary lifestyle. I certainly suspected that long before ever reading an article on it. And in 2005, I even dropped out of law school *partially* because I didn't want to be sitting at a desk all day. And yet, as a writer and coach, I spend a lot of time at my desk. Turns out, I spend the majority of my day seated after all! My schedule is more forgiving, though, so I can go for a walk or practice yoga, work out, take a five-minute dance break, or even go masturbate or booty call my man—when I have one—in the middle of the day.

But sometimes I'd get so absorbed staring at my computer screen that I'd forget I had those options. For many years, I may as well have been at a nine-to-five office job since I spent so much time sitting. But then I started reminding myself how important movement is all throughout the day. I started taking breaks to go for a walk or dance around, and it improved my energy level as well as my mood.

Can you relate to any of this? How much of *your* day is spent seated at a desk or on a couch? If you spend most of your time sitting, it may be helpful to set "movement reminders" or alarms on your phone or other device. Or use sticky notes or your day planner if that works better for you. Over time, you probably won't need the reminders because movement will just feel like a natural and welcome part of your daily flow. To get started, try scheduling something in before each meal, such as a five to ten-minute walk around the block or some jumping jacks, a little stretching, or dancing to your favorite song. Let frequent bursts of body movement become part of your daily life. One way to do that is with what Vanessa Nova, spiritual guide and healer, calls "five-minute dance parties."

Practice:

FIVE-MINUTE DANCE PARTY

Dancing is one of the best ways to drop into and express your feminine sexuality. In addition to being an enjoyable form of exercise, it's a wonderful way to let your Shakti flow! If you're thinking to yourself, *"But I don't know how to dance,"* don't worry. Just turn on the music and let it move you. If it feels strange at first, believe it will get easier, and more fun, over time.

Here's what you do: choose a song, play it, get up, and dance. Easy, right? You can do this once a day or whenever you need an energy boost.

I also recommend scheduling at least twenty-five to thirty minutes of cardio at least three to four times per week—and it can be something as simple as dancing or going for a short hike. But before you add that to your menu, check with your healthcare professional to make sure your body is healthy enough for rigorous activity. Cardio work is strenuous (and sweat-inducing), so you need that "all clear" before engaging in a new exercise routine. And don't worry if you have to work up to working out—simply going for a walk or practicing some qigong is an excellent way to build up to activities that boost your heart rate. Although you may not be sweating during them, you're still reaping the benefits of regular movement.

The point is to schedule in some cardio (or some form of movement) at least a few times a week, *but you don't have to stop there.* When I'm really following through on doing all the things I know will help me feel my best each day, I work out with a cardio DVD in the morning, and then in the middle of the day or early evening, I'll also go for a walk, even if just for five minutes. Once or twice a week, I also go dancing, and I practice Sheng Zhen Gong, do some jumping jacks, or dance around whenever the mood strikes me. This is *my* personal ideal, but I certainly do slack off at times (I mean, I am human, right?). Sometimes all I do is a few minutes of yoga or qigong and walk around the block, if anything.

The important thing for you to remember is to **move your body.** It's about creating a different lifestyle, one with more activity and body awareness. For example, if you usually sit on the couch to watch TV or movies, you can spend at least part of that time on a rebounder or some other sort of exercise equipment, like an elliptical, while getting your fix. This will help you kill two birds with one stone—or as my friend prefers to say, "feed two birds with one scone."

Plus, if you engage your senses with entertaining sights or sounds while working out, you're more likely to make these activities a regular part of your menu. So if you'd rather scrub your toilet with a toothbrush than walk on a treadmill or use a stationary bike, you could read a book or listen to your favorite music to make it more enjoyable. Or try listening to podcasts, radio shows, or audiobooks while you're exercising (or doing active household chores, like vacuuming). If what's in your ears has your full attention, you'll probably exercise even longer than you planned. Pretty cool, huh?

And as you become more in touch with and aware of your body and your deepest needs, you'll naturally want to move more. You won't be able to sit for long periods of time, and not out of having ADD or back pain; it'll be because you'll know better, and you'll stop suppressing your natural impulse to move.

Reconnect with Your Body's Wisdom

As children, this natural impulse is disciplined and trained right out of us. Whether it's in or out of the classroom, we're told, "Sit still! Stop moving around!" Children have a lot of energy. They're active and really in touch with their primal animal bodies, so it's natural for them to move a lot. But in order to function in society (and fit in as well), we're taught to suppress our natural desire for movement by well-intentioned teachers, parents, caregivers, and even the media. We're conditioned to suppress and control our energy. And while there are times and places that do require us to use a certain amount of restraint, I'm not a big fan of saying "that's inappropriate" because I think we should do what we feel (and, besides, who am I to judge?). However, there are times and places where it would definitely be impossible or seemingly inappropriate to jump around, shake, or stretch.

But being at your desk in your office, or even in the grocery store, is no excuse. Those aren't places where it's not okay to move around. And even if you're in a place where it's "inappropriate," consider excusing yourself to go to the bathroom. For example, let's say you're at church, a wedding, a business meeting, or in a movie theater. Just politely excuse yourself, so you can take a little break to jump around or shake it out. Or tell yourself that as soon as the thing is over, you'll be free to move around. But don't totally deny and suppress that urge; acknowledge it and honor it. Do something about it. Do something *with* it. Whether it's in the moment or saying to yourself, "Okay, yeah, we need some movement. Can't do it right now, but give me a half an hour or an hour, and I promise." And then keep that promise.

Setting Realistic Goals

Speaking of making promises you can keep, it's important to set realistic goals in terms of exercise and physical fitness. There are countless media images to compare yourself to and fitness advertisements promising dramatic results. My advice to you, though, is to focus on the results you get on the inside, and allow any external results, any changes in physical appearance, to be icing on the cake.

You also need to take care in terms of preventing injury or burnout. If something doesn't look safe or possible for you to do physically, don't do it. But don't give up, either. Just modify the movement. The best workout DVDs include somebody doing a modified version of the movements. Or, if you're working with a personal trainer, he or she can ensure your safety.

And now it's time for some goal setting.

Practice:

PHYSICAL FITNESS GOAL SETTING

Although I believe in the power of the mind and visualization, rather than fixating on how you want to look or setting a goal such as the number of pounds you want to lose or the dress size you want to fit into, start with just setting the goal of how often you'll be exercising. And then show up for it when you say you will.

Exercise type: *i.e., Dance*

Number of minutes: *i.e., 30 minutes or more*

Days of the week: *i.e., Sundays, Wednesdays, and Fridays*

Put this on your calendar and set reminders if needed. Prioritize your workout, stick with it, and you will feel better.

If you're including cardio *and* yoga or qigong, or even striving for all three, my advice to you is to start off by alternating days. Whenever you add a new activity, you want to give your body time to adapt to the change. If it's been a while since you did any type of regular exercise, you need to let your body get acclimated. Another option is to start off with only five to ten minutes of yoga or qigong in addition to your cardio routine (or non-cardio movement). This will prevent burnout or feelings of failure, and then you can build up to more days per week and/or more minutes per day.

Variety is fine; consistency is key. Just do something that gets your heart rate up, your blood flowing, and ideally something that helps you break a sweat unless you have a medical condition or injury that prevents that.

Movement and Cravings

One benefit of movement is that it can short-circuit cravings. If you're craving something you know is contributing to weight gain, bloating, or feeling sluggish, consider going for a walk. You can even tell yourself you can have the thing you're craving *after* the walk—if you still want it at that point. Or do something else you love, ideally something active, so you get the benefit of calorie-burning. Even though I never like to focus on counting calories consumed or burned, if you want to lose weight, calorie-burning activities will help. But mostly it's the **endorphins of exercise** I want you to focus on in terms of the benefits of movement. Why? Because it'll help you feel better about yourself and your choices.

Let's say you're craving something sweet or comforting, and then you go for a walk, and it feels really good, but you still want that ice cream or pizza. The difference is, now that desire is coming from a place of awareness. You're already feeling good because you've added some activity to your day, so any negative feelings you had that would've accompanied giving in to that quick fix of superficial energy have been squashed. If you're already feeling filled up in a deeper way, and then you give in to a craving, you'll probably eat less. And in terms of the caloric or fat intake, because you've just worked out, your metabolism will be higher, so you'll be burning it off more quickly.

The other possibility is that you might not even want that thing that you were craving after you go for that walk. To illustrate, here's a little story about something I experienced while in the midst of writing this book:

Today while making lunch, I did a few Orgasmic Breaths, and it just perked me up a little bit and made me feel more excited about the lunch I was preparing. The colors of the lettuce, of the greens, looked even more vibrant, and it felt pleasurable to my eyes. And yet when I sat to eat, I didn't feel as excited about my meal.

I wanted some other sense of stimulation, such as watching a TV show or checking email while eating. But I didn't do that. I just sat down to eat and gobbled it up quickly without chewing thoroughly.

Afterward, my energy was low and I was on the verge of feeling overwhelmed.

I had felt really inspired in the morning, but now I needed something to help me focus and hone in on what I wanted to do next in my day. And if I'd had any chocolate at home, I would have eaten it. Although that's totally acceptable, and sometimes highly recommended, I was glad I didn't have any. It gave me a chance to walk my talk in terms of the things we can do rather than giving in to the craving or quick fix.

Eating chocolate would have been a quick fix for what I really wanted—an energy burst and more clarity. I wanted inspiration. I wanted to feel refreshed, rejuvenated, revitalized. Chocolate may have made me feel good temporarily, on the surface level. But the depth, the deeper pleasure and rejuvenation, the refreshing feeling I wanted, I knew I could get by going for a walk on my favorite nearby trail. So I went for that walk and got exactly what I wanted out of it. No need for chocolate afterward.

See? It works. Whether it's a hike, a walk around the block, or a workout video, do whatever it takes to fill yourself up without binging or compulsive eating. Movement changes your perspective, so it's also a great way to short-circuit cravings and can be as simple as going for a walk, spinning around a few times, or doing some jumping jacks.

Practice:

JUMPING JACKS INSTEAD OF SNACKS

Jumping jacks are great in that they give you an energy boost and can alter your mood partially because of moving the arms above the head. It's healing for the Heart when we raise our arms up high. And as you know from earlier, when the Heart is open, qi flows better, and you feel more joy.

If you've never done jumping jacks before, here are the instructions:

First, stand with your feet together, knees slightly bent, and arms at your sides.

Then, jump while raising arms and separating legs out to the sides. Land on your feet with legs apart and arms overhead. Jump again while lowering arms and returning legs together. Land on feet with arms and legs in original position and repeat. Make sure knees slightly bend upon landing.

Note: If jumping is hard on you or not possible, you can try a seated form of jumping jacks in which you just raise your arms up and down over your head and leave the jumping out of it altogether. Any kind of movement will work for this; doing jumping jacks is just an example because it has a nice catchy ring to it—and because of the benefits mentioned above.

Another option for movement is qigong, especially Sheng Zhen Gong, which is truly one of the best things you can do for yourself. It combines movement and breath to help you exchange qi with the Universe. This results in you feeling *energized and filled up* with Love and vital life-force energy instead of empty calories.

Sexercise

Craving a different kind of movement? Something a little juicier (and orgasmic), perhaps? How about considering sex as a fun way to get more movement into your day? If you have a partner, the two of you can get more physical during lovemaking and consider that your exercise. If you're having sex with yourself, it may be hard to work up an actual sweat. However, you can at least explore bringing more movement into your masturbation session, whether it's stretching your legs or making larger pelvic movements. Taking a striptease, pole-dancing, or burlesque dance class can also be a fun, sexy way to work out. These classes not only make you work up a sweat, but also give you more confidence when engaging with a lover—or even with yourself!

Finding Activities You Enjoy

By now you know that it's important to move your body on a regular basis, cardio workouts or not. Find activities you enjoy and start engaging in them more often. If you enjoy popping in a cardio DVD, as I do, fantastic! But if you don't like things like workout DVDs or going to the gym, you can still find ways to get your heart rate up or at least do some gentle movements to get your energy flowing.

Remember, the idea here is to fill your day with things that bring you great joy, excitement, and pleasure, *and* to cultivate your qi and make sure your sexual energy is flowing. To prevent qi stagnation, it's crucial to get up and move around from time to time, so why not enjoy yourself? And as Master Li would say, "Enjoy the movements; enjoy your life." There is great wisdom in these words. Choose activities you enjoy or try something new that you've always been curious about. The only way to truly integrate movement into your life is to decide to enjoy what you do. You'll never form a new habit if you don't enjoy yourself. Love your activities, and they will help you feel happier and more fully alive.

NOW, TAKE A BREAK from reading to go for a walk, dance around, or practice some Sheng Zhen. And every day **move your body in ways that bring you joy and pleasure.**

Chapter 11

FOOD, FOOD, GLORIOUS FOOD

*"Part of the secret of success in life
is to eat what you like..."*

~ MARK TWAIN

Food, my dear, is a wonderful thing. Think about it. There are all these plants producing edible delights—some sweet, some salty, some bitter, some sour. Fruits, vegetables, grains, legumes, nuts, seeds—yum! An abundance of fresh delights for your taste buds and nourishment for your whole being. And if you're a meat or dairy eater, there are also all these animals sacrificing their lives to provide you with tasty, nourishing treats from their flesh and milk.

It truly is a treat to eat anything at all. From the shopping or the harvesting to the preparation to the cooking to the eating, and even to the digesting and eliminating, simply connecting more consciously with your food can be a way to enhance your enjoyment and satisfaction. It also leads to effortlessly making healthier choices. And what you eat and how you eat it is of the utmost importance to your well-being.

Food is foundational. We truly *are* what we eat. When the body is healthy and strong, it provides the optimal container for your soul and your spirit. Our bodies are temples, and what we put into them matters. However, in my opinion, dietary advice can feel disempowering if it focuses too specifically on what foods *to* eat and what foods *not* to eat. My aim is to empower you to tune in to your own body wisdom to hear your desires, wants, and needs.

I want you to see food as an opportunity for self-love, self-*pleasuring* even. But first, fill yourself up with *life*, with non-food sources of nourishment, and then the actual food part will come easier.

Filling the Void

Do you ever find yourself eating to fill a void, to not feel so empty? Perhaps you're aware that this is what you're doing. Perhaps you're not. I used to do this without thinking, and then I started doing it consciously. I didn't necessarily stop turning to comfort food. But when I did turn to it, I did so with awareness. I jokingly referred to it as "conscious unconscious eating."

But it's no joke. It's a self-defeating, self-destructive act when done in excess. Now, notice I say *when done in excess?* That's because, in order to be our healthiest and happiest, we must be self-compassionate and give ourselves permission to be the messy humans we are. Unless you have a serious need to be super strict, it's okay to sometimes eat something "unhealthy" or in excess. It's okay, until it's naturally not okay. What do I mean by "naturally not?" I mean that at some point, over time, you will want these junk foods—or as we're learning to call them, *comfort* foods— less and less. You will naturally eat less of them when you do partake. And perhaps, at some point, you will not even crave them at all.

It's my hope that this book is helping you understand that filling the void doesn't have to involve food, sex, or another person. Instead, you can fill that sense of emptiness with Love and **feel whole and complete.** Yes, we need others, and we need food, but happiness and a sense of fulfillment are primarily inside jobs.

Befriending Food

Sometimes it's hard to make changes to our diets because of an unhealthy relationship to food. Too often we view food as something that can make us fat or feel bloated or sick, cause a breakout, or give us gas, constipation, diarrhea, or parasites. Deciding what to eat can feel so complex at times, and when wrapped up in body image and emotional issues, it can just seem like a mess or a chore. Certainly not a delight. Certainly not a source of *pleasure* and something for which to be grateful.

But if you cultivate a new and healthy relationship with food, you will see results and improvements in your overall sense of well-being. Just as you are befriending your body and your own precious self through the practices in this book, it's also important to befriend your food. As your relationship with *yourself* improves and deepens, an improvement in your food choices will naturally follow. You'll feel more reverence and honor for your body, more care, as if feeding a child or making an offering to a goddess, and so it will be easier and more enjoyable to eat healthily.

Thanksgiving Every Day

I didn't grow up saying grace at the table, but sometimes I'd jokingly say, "Rub-a-dub-dub, thanks for the grub." Now, however, I see the importance of *sincerely* taking a moment of prayer or gratitude prior to a meal, and not just on Thanksgiving. If you are religious or spiritual and already in this habit, fantastic. Regardless of religion, spirituality, or lack thereof, if this feels triggering, get over it. Seriously. It doesn't need to be a religious act, although it can be if that resonates with you. All you're doing is saying thanks. Acknowledging. Appreciating. And as you thank this food you eat, in return, your food will serve you better.

Practice:

CULTIVATING AN ATTITUDE OF GRATITUDE

Option 1: Just say "thanks" before each meal. This can be a general thanks, or you can thank each and every ingredient in whatever it is you're eating. This serves a hidden purpose of heightening your awareness of ingredients in processed foods, even "healthy" processed foods like gluten-free crackers.

Option 2: In addition to saying thanks before commencing your meal, say thank you as a mantra with every bite or with each breath. Repeating "thank you" over and over again will help focus your attention in the present moment, calm your mind, relax your body, and amplify the positive effects of gratitude.

Cultivating an attitude of gratitude has been shown to improve psychological and physical health. Because a regular gratitude practice can alleviate anxiety or depression and result in a greater sense of fulfillment and happiness, I also encourage you to list five things every day for which you're grateful. You can start with just one. This can be written in a journal, or you can simply think about it when you wake up in the morning or before you sleep at night. As you go throughout your day, notice the little things for which you can be grateful. Count your blessings, and let each one light you up and tickle you with delight in the spirit of living a multi-orgasmic life.

Food Is Simple

There are so many dietary theories out there, many of which contradict one another. This makes food itself, and dietary advice, seem really complicated. But from my perspective, it's actually quite simple. The basics are:

- **Drink enough water.** It hydrates your body, improves elimination, gives you more energy, prevents false hunger, and helps give your skin its glow.

- **Eat more whole foods, especially vegetables.** Fiber fills you up and helps eliminate waste from the body. You'll get more nutrients than from processed foods and have more energy (plus veggies are better for your body and overall well-being).

- **Chew thoroughly.** Chewing thoroughly helps you slow down and breathe, which relaxes you and helps you feel full and eat less. Slow, mindful eating also improves digestion.

- **Avoid sugar and other processed foods.** If you do, you'll feel less bloated, increase your chances of losing weight, improve your emotional well-being as well as your skin, and decrease your risks of developing various types of disease.

That's it. End of story. Or at least it *can* be. As you befriend your body and experience more pleasure and comfort in your daily activities, it will be easier to make these changes to your diet. Remember that there are some variables when it comes to the way in which you eat, which foods are best for you, and which foods are harmful. But the above basics are a good place to start, as that *might* be all it takes, depending upon your goals and on your underlying associations with and relationship to food.

The thing is, it also takes support and practice. Most likely you have some habits around what you eat and some cravings that come on strong. Regardless of what you *know*, regardless of "knowing better," you still may find yourself eating in a way that isn't for your greatest good and doesn't leave you feeling very well. Although food itself is simple, your relationship with food—why and what and how you eat—may be more complex. And that's why it's important to begin with the self-love and mindfulness practices in this book. It's also important to be patient as you experiment with what works best for you.

Primary and Secondary Food

Food isn't the only thing that feeds us. One of the best things I learned in my Health Coach training at the Institute for Integrative Nutrition (IIN) is the concept of "primary food" and "secondary food." Secondary food is more about modern nutrition, such as looking at things like carbs and proteins and processed foods versus whole foods. Primary food goes much deeper and is what I would call "soul food," which can be found in many, if not all, of the following:

- Relationships
- Finances
- Career
- Creativity
- Joy
- Social Life
- Education
- Health
- Home Cooking
- Physical Activity
- Home Environment
- Spirituality

Joshua Rosenthal, founder of IIN, explains, "Sometimes we are fed not by food but by the energy in our lives." So how can we get you to a state of ecstasy in all these primary areas of your life? How can we feed your soul?

When you feel satisfied and happy with these primary foods, it becomes easier to make healthier secondary food choices. That is one reason why this book barely even talks about food and nutrition. Instead, I encourage you to find more fulfillment through other things such as heightened senses, conscious breathing, enhanced energy awareness, and your relationship with yourself.

Crowding Out

Another thing I learned at IIN was to tell my clients to start eating more healthy and nourishing foods, including greens and whole foods, as a way to "crowd out" the unhealthy or excessive comfort food. This approach helps prevent the backfiring associated with restrictive dieting.

Practice:

CROWDING OUT

Make a list of all the healthy foods you can think of and that you'd be willing to eat; if you're stumped, see Healthy Snacks and the Shopping List in Appendix 2 or just start listing various types of vegetables and nuts or seeds.

And take some time to consider that rather than restricting or cutting stuff out, you instead can focus on filling yourself and your life with what truly nourishes and satisfies you. You may even want to write down what comes to mind or refer back to your Pleasure List from chapter 3 or your alternatives list from the Triggers, Cravings, & Alternatives practice in chapter 9.

Although crowding out is meant to be about eating healthier foods to crowd out the unhealthy foods, this whole book is full of practices that will also help you "crowd out." But now it *is* time to focus on food. So I invite you to start adding more greens, more veggies, more whole foods and water into your diet. Doing so will help you fill yourself up, resulting in less room and less desire for things that aren't so good for you.

The Truth about Fats

When it comes to what's not so good for you, fatty foods may be one of the first things that comes to mind. Because of all the images of skinny women we're flooded with as well as information about obesity, there's a fear of fat that has developed. We're scared of it, even if just on a subconscious level. However, **the right kinds and amounts of fat are good for you.**

Luckily, fat has made a comeback over the years with more people learning about "good fats." Yet I still know plenty of overweight women who don't even want to eat those. And they're not getting any skinnier any faster by depriving themselves of this essential nutritional building block. As mentioned in an earlier chapter, fat is necessary for the healthy functioning of your body and your brain and is actually essential for you to have a healthy libido and the ability to orgasm. Learn to harness its positives, and let fat be your friend!

Aphrodisiacs

Another way to experience pleasure from food is to choose items that are considered to be aphrodisiacs. The more this book affects you, the more foods will turn you on as you'll find yourself feeling aroused by far more than ever before. You'll see things differently, and smell, taste, touch, and experience things in a new way. That being said, there are certain foods known to heighten libido and increase arousal and pleasure. Here is a list of some common aphrodisiacs:

Aphrodisiacs

Artichokes	Olive oil
Arugula	Oysters
Avocado	Pine nuts
Bananas	Pomegranate
Chai tea	Pumpkin seeds
Cherries	Red chili peppers
Chocolate	Strawberries
Figs	Watermelon
Honey	

Consider adding these foods into your diet to help you feel sexier and turned on throughout your day. And for specifics on why they are considered aphrodisiacs, visit the Resources section.

Inspired Cooking

Food preparation can be fun and pleasurable, even if it's just for one. It can be a time of self-care, self-love, and experimentation. It can be a meditation, an awareness practice. I want you to get to a point where you set aside enough time for each meal (or at least one meal a day or even one a week to start) so that you can really relax into and enjoy this time and check in with your body about what it wants. You can even think of meal time as a form of foreplay, self-love, or self-pleasuring. **Make love to yourself through feeding yourself the best and most nourishing foods** while also being fully present and not in a hurry.

When feeling uninspired or like meal time is a drag or a chore, try the Culinary Visualization practice.

Practice:

CULINARY VISUALIZATION

Take a deep breath and close your eyes.

Ask yourself, your body, what you want, what you need, what would be the best meal as a whole or the best ingredients to use.

Allow yourself to imagine the tastes, smells, and textures of the food. See yourself delighting in not only the eating of it, but also in the preparation. See yourself with a radiant glow, a smile, and feeling happy and fulfilled.

Allow your body to relax and open, maybe even breathing into your nipples and/or your yoni.

When you start off mealtime with a practice like this, feeling happy and inspired, maybe even sexually excited, you're more likely to choose what's truly best for you and to enjoy your eating experience. The trick for effectiveness is consistency and commitment. You can experiment by adding this to your menu and seeing what happens. Doing a little Sheng

Zhen Gong or other movement practice before a meal or snack can also help you feel happy and fulfilled prior to eating, as can many of the practices within *The Multi-Orgasmic Diet*.

Blood Sugar and Snacking

As you know, sometimes you need a little something in between meals. But occasionally you might just need to trade in that treat for some jumping jacks, a few conscious breaths, or a good ol' self-pleasuring session. Often, those options, or some Orgasmic Breaths and saying, "Mmmmm, yes, oh god, yes!" can make you laugh and perk you up enough to snap you out of an anxiety-induced or void-filling desire to snack.

It's also wise to drink some water when you get a craving to first see if you're dehydrated. If after the water and any of those activities, you still really need a little something, that's fine. Go ahead. But consider setting alarms on your phone or computer if you need help remembering to drink more water. You can also see if adding more protein or more nourishing whole foods helps reduce cravings and the need to eat between meals.

The thing about snacking, though, is that some people really do best in terms of energy level and blood sugar if they eat in between their regular meals. For most of my life, I thought being a grazer was the healthiest choice. But I recently realized that I was never giving my digestive system a rest during my waking hours. I began considering this when I realized that I was feeling abnormally tired and low on energy despite all the "healthy" and "right" things I was doing throughout the day in terms of diet, awareness practices, and exercise. So I stopped grazing and began having three satisfying meals per day.

I still usually have a snack in the afternoon and evening, but I'm no longer reaching for food every couple of hours as I had been for years. And guess what? It helped to really take the time for breakfast, lunch, and dinner, to prepare and eat a substantial meal that was meant to carry me through for three to four hours rather than just two. I felt more grounded, more focused, and less tired. I also had fewer cravings, and when I did give in to one, I didn't need as much.

If you've been a grazer, try this: give your system a rest. Eat every three to four hours instead of every two. And don't skip meals, especially breakfast. It's really important to eat! To give yourself fuel! Even if you're sedentary, such as with an office job, your brain runs on glucose and needs you to eat to fuel it.

And if possible, don't eat anything after 8 p.m. The liver needs time to just chill, and people who follow this rule tend to see a flatter belly and faster results when it comes to losing weight. But if you do need something in the evening because of low blood sugar, let it just be a spoon of nut butter or something that won't fill you up but will help you feel grounded, so you can sleep well without blood sugar issues or hunger waking you in the middle of the night.

Breaking the Fast

Speaking of waking up, how do you start your mornings? Do you take time to nurture and nourish yourself? Hopefully, if you've gotten this far in this book, you have been taking time in the mornings to be good to you. But is part of being good to you making sure you eat a healthy breakfast?

Please do break the fast each morning, as it helps prevent low blood sugar, adrenal fatigue, and poor eating choices later in the day. If you're not a breakfast eater, you can start off slow and small and easy; you can just make a protein shake or grab a banana, protein bar, or hard-boiled egg (boil up a batch in advance so they're readily available). Whatever it is, just make yourself eat something—for now, *anything* is fine. And if that "anything" is a donut, give yourself some time to find a healthier option. Breakfast truly is the most important meal. It's foundational for the rest of your day.

If you don't usually have an appetite in the mornings, give yourself time to develop one and to see how it affects your energy level and mood. If you're not used to eating breakfast, it might actually seem unhelpful at first, but you need to allow an adjustment period. It's absolutely crucial to eat breakfast to prevent overeating and making other unhealthy food choices later in the day.

There are other diets and detox programs that say it's okay not to eat breakfast and to go for a really long time without eating. But for optimal stability and pleasure, I say don't deprive yourself of breakfast. Rushing around in the morning, not taking the time to feed and to nurture and nourish yourself, goes against what we're working toward here: living a life in which you **love yourself enough to treat yourself like the goddess you are and take care of yourself like your most beloved lover or child.** Would you deny your child breakfast? No. That would be considered abuse. So be good to yourself; feed your inner child with a healthy breakfast every single day.

Repression and the Stomach

On a related note, don't deny your hunger. Women have been programmed to repress their desires, both for food and for sex, and, really, in general. And the same messages that create this repression can also dampen the experience of pleasure when eating, having sex, or participating in any other activity. When you give in to a craving for chocolate or ice cream, a masturbation break or a booty call, enjoy it! View it as a gift you're giving yourself, an honoring of your desire and something in which to truly delight.

This was something I had to remind one of my Get Your Groove Back coaching clients about while I was writing this book. She came to me for a CranioSacral and SomatoEmotional Release session to help her with sleep. However, one of the premises of CranioSacral therapy is for the practitioner to be grounded, present, and neutral, with no agenda. Even though there was the intention to focus on sleep, there was also the understanding that we'd see what her body needed. And her body needed us to give her stomach some attention.

After a technique called diaphragmatic release, my hands moved over slightly and were gently sandwiching her stomach. I felt compelled to ask my client about her relationship with her stomach, specifying I was referring to the organ, not the belly in general. This question led to a substantial dialogue and further inquiry that revealed her stomach was tired of not being listened to and tired of so much repression. Her stomach wanted more freedom. Her stomach was hungry.

And guess what happened after the session? She started eating more, and her mood and sleep improved! So remember, even if there's a need or desire to lose weight, it's important not to starve or punish yourself by withholding and repressing. Free yourself, woman! Live it up!

And now? Let's put it all together . . .

Chapter 12

PUTTING IT ALL TOGETHER ~ THE PLAN, THE MENU, THE LIFE

"Count your orgasms, not your calories."
~ THE GODDESS REBELLION

Congratulations! Whether you've already been engaging in the practices along the way or not, you've come so far. Even just by reading the previous chapters, you may have noticed a shift in perspective and in how you feel. Maybe even in how you appear. Have you already started exuding more of a radiant glow or developed a twinkle in your eye? Have you already started slimming down or simply feeling better in your body? Are you smiling more?

Wherever you are in your journey right now is perfect. In this chapter, you will see more clearly how to fully implement the Multi-Orgasmic Diet by living a multi-orgasmic life! This chapter will help you maximize your experience and results.

Are you ready??

Let's do this!

The Full Menu

Because it's important to take personal uniqueness into consideration, I firmly believe in *not* prescribing one set diet plan or menu options for readers in general. Therefore, I'm providing a *sample* menu instead as well as a list of menu items from which you may pick and choose. You may also add to this list. And the items on this menu? By now, you know that they won't be food. Instead, they are practices designed to help you cultivate and connect to your sexual energy, awaken your senses, relax and open yourself to feeling more pleasure and feeling more fully alive so that you can make healthier choices that allow you to enjoy and feel good about what you eat, *whatever* you eat.

Here is your sample menu. You can change the order and pick and choose what works best for you. Remember to be consistent and committed but also *playful* with this experiment. Refer to the templates at www.rebeccacliogould.com/bookbonus for menus, contracts, and observation forms.

5-DAY SAMPLE MENU

Unless otherwise indicated, these practices are to be done prior to eating, if possible, rather than while eating. And the snack suggestions can either replace or just precede your snack of choice.

Please note: When eating, slowing down and chewing thoroughly is always recommended. To help with this, you can shut your eyes at the beginning of each meal or snack, or whenever you notice you are starting to eat faster, and take a few mindful breaths.

DAY 1

Breakfast: Masturbation or sex**

Snack: Eye-Gazing With Yourself in bathroom mirror or handheld mirror

Lunch: Orgasmic Breaths 10x (three **minimum**)

Snack: Jumping Jacks Instead of Snacks or Five-Minute Dance Party

Dinner: Save Room for Breath

Dessert: Heavenly Petting

DAY 2:

Breakfast: Eye-Gazing With Yourself

Snack: Masturbation or Cop a Feel

Lunch: Gathering Qi or Bouncy Shake

Snack: Five-Minute Dance Party or Multi-Orgasmic Walk

Dinner: Hand Caress

Dessert: Taste Yourself

DAY 3:

Breakfast: Masturbation or Sex

Snack: Bouncy Shake or Gathering Qi

Lunch: Nipple Breathing

Snack: Chocolate Offering to the Goddess (doesn't have to be chocolate, could be rosewater mist or a glass of water)

Dinner: Orgasmic Organs

Dessert: Happy Foods

DAY 4:

Breakfast: Sheng Zhen (i.e., first three movements or all of Awakening the Soul)

Snack: Lotus Flower Breathing

Lunch: Multi-Orgasmic Meal

Snack: Orgasmic Breaths 10x (three **minimum**)

Dinner: Let the Horizon Come to You (if driving home or out for dinner) or Full-Body Relaxation

Dessert: A Night of Sensual Self-Pleasuring

DAY 5:

Breakfast: Eye-Gazing With Yourself

Snack: Multi-Orgasmic Walk or Orgasmic Breaths

Lunch: Masturbation or Sex

Snack: Bouncy Shake or Sheng Zhen

Dinner: Culinary Visualization

Dessert: Foot Massage or Play with Your Hair

**Anytime sex or masturbation is listed, please know that you don't need to do that if you're not in the mood. Follow your feeling; you can give yourself a foot massage or use some other self-pleasuring practice instead. Also, no need for experiencing a peak orgasm each day or multiple times a day; focus more on cultivating and circulating your sex energy, awakening your senses, opening your Heart, and feeling good!

Tip: If this all looks like too much variety, you can repeat the same practices each day or just start with something like using Orgasmic Breaths or Gathering Qi before every meal and snack. You can even start with just one meal and/or snack per day.

The truth is, I recommend starting every morning with Eye-Gazing with Yourself, repeating "Today I intend to love like I've never been hurt," practicing some Sheng Zhen Gong, and using Orgasmic Breaths or a walk outside when unhealthy cravings come on. But I know that might be too much to ask of you, especially in the beginning. Keep in mind that the above menu is a sample that offers plenty of variety as you experiment with what's best for you. If fewer snacks or fewer practices feels better, just update your menu plan accordingly.

Create Your Own Plan

On that note, I highly suggest you create your own plan. You can modify the menu online at www.rebeccacliogould.com/bookbonus. For quick reference, I've included a comprehensive list of practices for your personalized Multi-Orgasmic Diet menu. As you look it over, ask yourself:

- What grabs me?
- What feels easiest to start implementing?

- What feels challenging, but in a good way?
- To what will I, and to what can I, truly commit?

Some of the options below are specific practices from this book that would make sense as menu items, some are included in the bonus materials, and some are simply things like taking a bubble bath or rubbing your belly.

Take a look at the menu options and see if you want to modify the sample meal plan or just start your own from scratch.

MULTI-ORGASMIC DIET MENU OPTIONS

Please note: This is a list of practices that make the most sense as actual menu items. This is not a complete list of every practice in the book. For that, see Appendix 1, which includes a comprehensive list sorted by chapters, with page numbers.

Arousal Allowance & Awareness

Ask for Some Sweetness

Assessing Your Needs

Awakening the Soul

Awareness of Breath

Be Sweet to Yourself

Befriending Fat

Befriending Your Body

Befriending Your Organs

Bouncy Shake

Breathing beyond the Nose, beyond the Lungs

Breathing into Your Nipples

Bubble Bath

Chew Your Way to Sweetness

Chocolate Offering to the Goddess

Culinary Visualization

Cultivating an Attitude of Gratitude

Delight in "Being Bad"

Eating with Your Eyes Closed

Enjoying the Silence & Listening to Yourself

Eye-Gazing with Yourself

Feel the Qi

Feeling & Releasing Your Feelings

Five-Minute Dance Party

Fondling & Flirting with Yourself

Foot Massage

Full-Body Breast Massage

Full-Body Relaxation & Energy Flow

Gathering Qi

Get Creative

Go for a Walk

Good Vibrations

Hand Caress

Happy Foods

Hearing Music Everywhere

Heavenly Petting

Identifying Deeper Cravings

Intend to Love Like You've Never Been Hurt

Intuitive Eating

Jumping Jacks instead of Snacks

Let the Horizon Come to You

Lotus Flower Breathing

Massage Bliss

Masturbation

Meditate

Multi-Orgasmic Meal

Multi-Orgasmic Walk

Multiple Mouthgasms

Night of Sensual Self-Pleasuring

Nurturing Your Inner Child

Opening to Pleasure

Orgasmic Breath

Orgasmic Organs

Penetrative, Receptive, & Neutral Gaze

Permission Slips

Physical Fitness Goal Setting

Play with Your Breath

Play with Your Food

Play with Your Hair

Pleasure in the Palms of Your Hands

Pleasure List (refer to it)

Positive Brainwashing (a.k.a. Affirmations)

Rub Your Belly

Run Your Fingers through Your Hair

Save Room for Breath

Saying Yes to Life

Scent of a Woman

Self-Love Affirmations

Self-Massage

Sex

Sex Energy Circulation

Sensual Awakening practice by Lisa Schrader (book bonus)

Sheng Zhen mantra ("I am a big body of Love, full of qi, full of Love")

Sheng Zhen Gong ~ a whole form (series of movements)

Slowly Entering the Temple

Smell Your Food

Spray Yourself with Rosewater

Support System

Tasting Yourself

Tension Inventory & Full-Body Relaxation

Triggers, Cravings, & Alternatives (refer to list)

Unrestrained   The Yes Breath

Vocalizing Pleasure

If the options feel overwhelming, just relax. It's okay to choose only one practice to start. Whatever feels best for you. **This is your life, your choice. Experiment. Have fun with it. You got this.** And remember to utilize the online bonuses to help ensure your success!

A Simplified Plan

I also want to give you a simplified way to put this all into effect with something I call "5 for 5": **choose five practices and commit to five days,** and after those five days, commit to another five days. That can take some of the pressure off. Just five days at a time, repeated over and over and over again.

As you've already seen, there is an abundance of practices in this book. You don't *need* to use them all. What's likely to be most effective is to consistently use a handful of practices that resonate the most for you, on a regular basis, over a period of time.

What period of time? Recall from chapter 1 that it actually takes an average of more than twenty-one days to create a new habit; some say sixty-six is the new magic number. Therefore, I'm giving you two options here:

1. Commit to sixty-six days or more, right off the bat; or
2. Commit to five days at a time, aiming to renew that commitment at least twelve times after the initial five-day period.

Of course, you may instead commit to some other time period, like ninety days, or one week or month rather than five days at a time. How you go about it really depends on your personality, your lifestyle, what your personal goals and needs are, what type of support system you have (i.e., your family, friends, therapist, coach, etc.), and what types of promises you can make—and keep—when it comes to implementing new practices. It's crucial to **set yourself up for success and sustainable change,** and that includes making realistic promises so that you can trust yourself and feel good about keeping your word along the way.

If you want to start off with the 5 for 5 approach, I've provided a sample plan; feel free to swap out the practices below for other practices by accessing your online template or just writing it out yourself.

5 FOR 5

Breakfast: Eye Gaze with Yourself when you wake up in the morning

Mid-morning Snack (if needed): Orgasmic Breaths

Lunch: Bouncy Shake or Gathering Qi before lunch

Afternoon Snack: Orgasmic Breaths again

Dinner: Multi-Orgasmic Walk (even if just around the block), or Multi-Orgasmic Meal*

Dessert: Masturbation or Foot Massage

*If not using the Multi-Orgasmic Meal practice, do close your eyes for at least a few bites of at least one meal or snack every day.

Please note: If you skip more than two days, then you need to start over; never let more than two days pass. Allow it to slide if you *occasionally* skip one day. But do you even really want to skip a single day of self-love and pleasure practices? Maybe you skip a day or two of one practice, but not of another. Always do *something*, even if it's just three Orgasmic Breaths when a craving comes on, Gathering Qi once before each meal, or ten seconds of sincere, deeply intentional Eye-Gazing with Yourself in the morning.

A Couple of Important Notes Regarding These Menus

Not everyone eats three meals a day (though I recommend it), and not everyone will snack three times a day. These menu plans are just examples. You don't need to use the mid-morning snack, afternoon snack, and evening dessert spots. So modify the online templates as needed.

And please note that the practices are to be incorporated into your life *before* each meal or snack, unless it's a practice to be done *while* eating (i.e., Chew Your Way to Sweetness). **Please do not replace actual meals with practices.** Instead, use a practice when you wake up or right before breakfast, and then eat some actual food! I only recommend practices taking the place of food when it comes to snacking, and only if that works with your blood sugar and dietary needs. Sometimes we need to snack, but the practice will help us make a healthier choice or eat less of whatever we choose to indulge in.

Layering

If the simplified plan still looks like too much, you're not sure what you can handle, or you already know you need to ease into this, then a layering approach might work best for you. Perhaps you've already started layering, as was suggested in chapter 1.

In a layering approach, during the first week, you do just one or two new things, and then in week two, you add another practice or two into the mix, and so on. For example:

THE LAYERING APPROACH

- **Week 1:** Commit to three to ten Orgasmic Breaths before *at least* one meal per day or when cravings arise.

- **Week 2:** Continue with the breaths, and add in Eye-Gazing with Yourself each morning.

- **Week 3:** Continue with the breaths and eye-gazing, and now add in Full-Body Breast Massage.
- **Week 4:** Continue with breaths, eye-gazing, and self-massage. Add in Hand Caress or Masturbation at least a few times a week if not daily.

You get the point? You'll still need to commit and write it out for optimal success. But you have options and can take it at your own pace. It's all about experimentation and what works best, so you can either start off by strictly following one of the sample plans I've provided and then modify it if needed, or you can pick and choose for yourself from the start.

Sticking with It

What's important is to stick with the practices long enough for them to deeply work their magic and feel like a part of your life, a way of living and being. This might mean "less is more" in terms of how many practices to include in your diet. If my generic plan feels like too much variety for you, too many *different* practices, just use a few instead. Depending on your goals, you may even opt for using the practices only when cravings come on instead of at specified meal and snack times. Using a simplified plan will still give you results in less than sixty-six days, but sixty-six days or more will really help drive it in.

Getting one-on-one or group coaching is also a great way to help you clarify what handful of practices is best for you as an individual and/or when swapping out for another one would be wise. Coaching can also help you stick to the plan for long enough to see lasting results, but committing to yourself may be all it takes. And hopefully you'll enjoy the practices so much that you'll feel called to engage in some of these energy-cultivating, sensory-stimulating self-love and self-pleasuring practices beyond the sixty-six days as part of a new lifestyle.

Seven Essential Practices

Speaking of the abundance of practices and simplifying, I've created a list of what I personally consider to be the most essential practices to engage in on a regular basis. Some of the practices in the book are best for one-time or occasional use or just for a certain period of time. The following practices, however, are good habits to acquire as part of your ongoing wellness and self-care routine. Although I call these practices "essential," please know that **you do not need to do all of them in order to get results.** They are simply *my* personal favorites as well as what I've seen work best for those who prefer less variety. I also picked them because the whole list may seem overwhelming, and these options will benefit you the most while you're first finding your way. You can layer these in over time or just pick one or two or three and ignore the rest. It's up to you.

1. **Eye-gaze with yourself in the mirror.** But go beyond the eyes, also looking at your face. Admire your face. Always find something you like. Make yourself smile. Think loving thoughts as you gaze at your reflection. Start and/or end your day with this. I prefer doing it in bed with a hand mirror, but doing it in the bathroom (or any other) mirror is fine. See chapter 8.

2. **Breathe.** Take ten conscious breaths. Or even as few as three for a quicker little reset or boost anytime throughout the day. I love using the Orgasmic Breaths when I'm feeling low on energy or craving comfort food. I also use it sometimes when I'm being too mental, when I'm all in my head, stressing out or obsessing over something. As Tantra teacher David Cates says, "Trade in that thought for a breath." And it works! When Cates said it, the breathing technique he taught involved a long, deep, slow breath followed by making sound on the exhalation, like a loud sigh or "ha" sound. And he recommended three breaths. You can certainly do that, too, for stress relief and to quiet obsessive thoughts. But for stimulating that sex energy and perking yourself up with a sexy glow, the Orgasmic Breaths, those shorter breaths in and out through the mouth, are what do the trick—better than a cup of coffee. See chapter 6.

3. **Shakti Malan's Lotus Flower Breathing.** Get in the practice of relaxing the body and mind while intentionally connecting with your sex center, with your yoni. By just relaxing the body, energy will flow better. You may even feel aroused. This practice helps you cultivate receptive, feminine sexual energy and develop a deeper relationship with your yoni. In addition to strengthening self-love, you'll strengthen your PC muscles, both of which can intensify orgasm. See chapter 8.

4. **Sensual Eating, especially with eyes closed.** Eating with your eyes closed will help you slow down, breathe more, and chew better. This sort of mindful eating will help you experience more satisfaction and pleasure in your eating experience. You'll also discover that some of the foods you may have once enjoyed or craved aren't so good when you really take the time to truly taste them in a slow, conscious, savoring way.

   For example, I once ordered my favorite Thai food dish, ate it with my eyes closed, and didn't like it—except for the occasional pea. In the same vein, you might find yourself enjoying food you hadn't really thought of as delicious or delightful or sweet in the past. But the more you slow down and breathe and chew, the more certain foods will release their flavor and sweetness.

   Also, when you eat, think about making an offering to your temple (your body) and to the goddess that you are.

5. **Sheng Zhen.** Developing a Sheng Zhen practice is one of the most important things you can do for yourself, and it also might be the most challenging to schedule in and stick to. Then again, it might be easy. Trust me when I tell you this practice is powerful, a game changer, a life changer, a life saver. If you commit to sixty-six days of Sheng Zhen, or even just thirty days—heck, even just a week—you'll see why a regular practice of this unique Heart-opening qigong is crucial. When you open your Heart, qi flows better, which helps blood flow better, and both of these help you feel more alive, more turned on, more radiant.

   Plus, there's the Sheng Zhen mantra: "I am a big body of Love. Full of qi, full of Love." When you consciously connect with this message on a daily basis, even if not doing the movements, whether just once a day or all throughout your day, you'll simply feel better. You'll be smiling more without even realizing it. And people are attracted to that. You'll be more attractive. You'll be more in the flow. And all of that will help you feel happy and fulfilled, thereby preventing unhealthy eating patterns. Plus, as a bonus, some say qigong is good for your metabolism as well!

For more on Sheng Zhen and to find videos and other products, please visit the Resources page.

6. **Masturbation or other forms of self-pleasuring through touch.** Depending on your mood, your libido, and whether you have sufficient privacy, this might be more about just simply touching yourself than about bringing yourself to climax. Caress your body, feel your skin. Get yourself off, whether as a quickie before getting out of bed or during a lunch break or in a lengthier self-pleasuring session that you might even schedule into your calendar, like a date with yourself. Personally, I like to be more spontaneous with it. But I see value in scheduling in longer sessions, too, especially if you're a busy lady. Perhaps schedule in a long self-lovemaking session once a week. And then on other days, just have shorter moments of sweet self-touch or spicy masturbation.

7. **Intend to Love Like You've Never Been Hurt.** Start with committing to one week, but then recommit for another week and another and another with this as your daily mantra: "Today I intend to love like I've never been hurt." Think of this not only in terms of loving others, but also in terms of loving yourself. Not only will it impact your interactions with others, but it will free up your own innocence, that inner child, that bubble of joy and love, openness and curiosity. You will glow and feel more at peace. See chapter 5.

There you have it. If you feel overwhelmed by the number of practices in this book, just refer to the list above. Start with these, or even stick with them and forget about everything else. And I repeat, no need to use all seven of these. You can modify the menus in this chapter to include whichever practices you like. You can even use the same practice before every meal or snack. Ultimately, it's up to you. It's your choice.

Staying Committed and In the Flow

What will you do to stay committed and in the flow, to ensure you continue to implement the practices and teachings of this book in your life? Revisit chapter 1, if needed, to clarify your goals and commitments and support system. And remember to check out the MOD Facebook group or contact me if you would like to explore the possibility of one-on-one or group coaching. Starting a book club or Meetup group can also be a fun way to formulate a support and accountability system while meeting like-minded women; see Appendix 3 for how to do so. And perhaps most importantly, I encourage you to relax with this. **Be committed, but allow it to be easy, gentle, and enjoyable for you.** Drop into your feminine sexuality and sensuality by slowing down and not pushing yourself so hard.

Making Love to Life

The menu plans above, and all the material in this book, are designed to help you create a lifestyle in which you let every part of your day be an opportunity for intense enjoyment and excitement (a.k.a. "*orgasmic*"). When you wake up in the morning, delight in the comfort of your bed. Be grateful for another day. Look at yourself in the mirror and fill with self-love. Let every drop of shower water feel like sweet, tiny kisses. Spray yourself with rosewater; let it open your Heart. Massage yourself from head to toe. Make a sacred offering to your temple when you break the fast.

Notice all the sights and sounds and smells and tastes and opportunities for pleasurable touch as you go throughout your day, experiencing mouthgasms and Heartgasms and eargasms and . . . orgasms. Feel orgasmic energy flowing through you multiple times a day, wherever you are and whatever you're doing. Channel it into your creativity and other endeavors. Treat others, and yourself, with love and adoration, compassion, and patience. Relax and slow down. Delight in lingering in the valleys and in reaching the peaks. See the potential of everything and everyone as a lover, as a partner, as a source of fulfillment and pleasure. Tap into the energy that's all around you and inside of you. Fill yourself up. Make love to life! And live turned on.

Turned On ~ *a poem by Anto Ferrante*

Let's live turned on
Turn on your awareness
Turn on your senses
Turn on your desire

Let's live turned on
From dusk to dawn
Bring your intentions to life
Allow yourself to be the realization of your dreams

Let's live turned on
Bring your stamina up
Fill your dopamine tank to full
Seek your next adventure

Let's live turned on
May your eyes shine the light of the awakened
May your intentions bring love and well-being to all of us
May your actions be the realization of your Voice

Let's live turned on
Bring your playfulness to life
Let your innocence show you the way
Make your Divine Eros your guide

Let's live turned on
Wherever and whatever you are, live turned on
Limited and precious is the time you have to
manifest your full potentials
Do you know what they are?

Let's live turned on
Listen, sit, breathe
Your Voice will speak to you
And teach you to inquire and bring you insights

Let's live turned on
It's all a matter of practice
Just don't stop

Acknowledgments

The first acknowledgment I'd like to make is to you—you who chose to read this book. Thank you for your interest, your curiosity, your commitment, and also for trusting in me as a guide on this journey.

Creating this book was also a journey, and I'd like to thank the practices themselves and all the words that came through. Thanks to the gentle but loud whisperings in my Heart and my head, saying *now, do this now.* And thanks to everyone who supported me, encouraged me, and inspired me along the way. From acquaintances on social media to my closest friends and family, from clients and students to colleagues and teachers, you all had a part in this. There are too many to list, but you know who you are. And I thank you for having an impact on my life, and therefore on this book.

Special thanks to Tracy Teel. Tracy, you are a fantastic editor. I learned a lot from working with you both in the developmental edit phase and the copy editing and line editing phase. Thank you for your words of wisdom, sense of humor, answering my crazy long lists of questions, and for your beautiful line edits that made my "already good" writing even better. Thank you for being just the editor and the hand-holder I needed as a first-time author.

Speaking of hand-holding, special thanks to Kristen Tate for marketing and book launch support, in addition to proofreading. I deeply appreciate your help with navigating through this process. Thanks for being a trusted advisor and my behind-the-scenes self-publishing angel.

I'd also like to thank Sheila Parr for a beautiful book cover and interior book design. I know this wasn't the easiest job, with me combining two genres that usually aren't combined! And I truly appreciate your willingness and ability to come up with a variety of covers until we got it just right.

And thanks to Lori Draft for your edits and helping me integrate a few tricky changes that were needed while you were working with my manuscript.

I'm also grateful to those who read my manuscript before the professional editing phase: Ellison James, Michelle Hefner, Kim Eubanks, Kamala Chambers, Sasha Bishop, and Meg Hunter. Thank you for taking the time to read and to provide valuable feedback. All of you not only helped me improve my manuscript, but also confirmed I wasn't delusional—that what I'd written was already pretty darn good!

Special thanks to Bess O'Connor and Well Spirit Collective for believing in me and my book. I appreciate all your help with PR and spreading the word! Thank you, Miranda Aponte, for your support too.

A special thanks as well to everyone who directly contributed a practice to this book, or approved of a modified version: Shakti Malan, Lisa Schrader, Marcia Baczynski, Betty Martin, Laura Lavigne, Kamala Chambers, Vanessa Nova, Master Li Junfeng, and the Institute for Integrative Nutrition. And an additional thanks to Kamala for blessings on using her "living turned on" phrase and putting my own spin on it.

And on that note, thank you, Anto Ferrante for contributing your beautiful poem, "Turned On." It truly felt like the perfect end to this book!

Thanks to some fellow authors who provided guidance, encouragement, and support in various ways: Jenny D'Angelo, Dhebi DeWitz, Iva Nasr, and Jeff Brown.

Thanks to Jamie Batiste for helping out with the audio files for Lisa Schrader's book bonus.

Thank you, Matthias Rose, for pointing out the "symphony of sound" during a Multi-Orgasmic Meal in a busy restaurant!

Thanks to Noe Khalfa for enlightening me about the whole sixty-six days to change a habit thing. Your Worth the Journey group was also supportive.

Thanks to Christine Kloser for your Get Your Book Done program. It came into my life at just the right time to help me write this book that was demanding to be prioritized and written. Thank you, Carolin Hauser, for suggesting it.

I also want to acknowledge a couple of accountability buddies I had during the final phases of this process. PJ Harris and Shannon Soldo, thanks for holding me accountable!

Thanks to everyone who wasn't mentioned here, but whose name appears in this book.

And finally, I want to thank my parents and my brother. I feel blessed to not only love my parents, but to like them, and to consider my brother as one of my best friends. Thank you, Mom, Dad, and Daniel, for all of your love and support. Thanks for believing in me and also for pleasantly surprising me by your reactions when I revealed the title of the top secret project I'd been working on for months!

It truly takes a village to birth a book. And I am so grateful to you all.

RESOURCES

Please note: The content of this page can also be found online, with clickable links, at www.rebeccacliogould.com/bookresources.

Book Bonuses: www.rebeccacliogould.com/bookbonus

Awakening the Soul video: www.rebeccacliogould.com/videos

Addressing Trauma

There are various therapists, healing modalities, and books that can help you with trauma. If you are going to work with a therapist or healer, it is important to work with someone who is well-trained and trustworthy. Some resources I recommend are:

- *Waking the Tiger* by Peter Levine explores not only what trauma is but also provides steps on how to heal trauma.
- Somatic Experiencing® is a body-oriented approach to the healing of trauma and other stress disorders. More information can be found at www.traumahealing.org.
- EMDR: Information on Eye Movement Desensitization and Reprocessing can be found at www.emdria.org.
- SomatoEmotional Release (SER): SomatoEmotional Release is something that may or may not occur spontaneously during CranioSacral Therapy. Please visit www.upledger.com for more information.
- Pelvic Floor Physical Therapy and Rehabilitation: This may be useful if you've experienced any sort of trauma to the pelvic floor, which can be present for a variety of reasons, including sexual assault, childbearing, or even a slip-and-fall accident. To

explore this, look for a physical therapist who has had extensive training (not just a weekend workshop) in vaginal massage and treating pelvic pain. Please visit www.hermanwallace.com, www.womenshealthapta.org, or www.wildfeminine.com for more information and to find a therapist in your area. You may also find a practitioner through the Barral Institute: www.barral institute.com.

Books You Might Like to Explore

- *The Multi-Orgasmic Woman: How Any Woman Can Experience Ultimate Pleasure and Dramatically Enhance Her Health and Happiness*, by Mantak Chia and Rachel Carlton Abrams, M.D.
- *Sexual Awakening for Women* by Dr. Shakti Mari Malan
- *Healing Love Through the Tao: Cultivating Female Sexual Energy* by Mantak Chia and Maneewan Chia
- *The Orgasmic Diet: A Revolutionary Plan to Lift Your Libido and Bring You to Orgasm* by Marrena Lindberg
- *Full-Body Presence: Learning to Listen to Your Body's Wisdom* by Suzanne Scurlock-Durana
- *Tantra: The Path of Ecstasy* by Georg Feuerstein
- *The Function of the Orgasm: Sex-Economic Problems of Biological Energy* by Wilhelm Reich, translated by Vincent R. Carfagno
- *The New InterCourses: An Aphrodisiac Cookbook* by Martha Hopkins and Randall Lockridge
- *Road to Love: Lessons & Love Letters from a Journey to Intimacy* by Kamala Chambers
- *The Love Yo'Self Coloring Book* by Sara Young

More About Sheng Zhen and How to Find a Teacher or Obtain Instructional DVDs

Please visit www.shengzhen.org to find more information and the online store. DVDs can be ordered through the primary website or downloaded at www.vimeo.com/shengzhen/vod_pages.

There are also videos online at www.youtube.com/ShengZhenSociety.

If there are no teachers in your area, consider traveling to attend Master Li's workshops. You may also contact me for private instruction via Skype or Google Hangout or for a referral to another teacher.

Additional Resources

Visit www.rebeccacliogould.com/bookresources for links to articles, products, and more information on the following:

- Adding more whole foods to your diet
- Aphrodisiacs
- Aromatherapy
- Body positivity
- Cuddle party ~ a safe space for your touch needs
- Eating disorders and disordered eating
- Laura Lavigne's "Essence Cards Deck"
- Qi, Jing, and Shen
- Mantak Chia's "Inner Smile"
- Rebirthing and other forms of breathwork
- Sexological bodyworkers
- "Why is Sex Sacred?" Article by Dr. Deborah Taj Anapol

Appendix 1

LIST OF PRACTICES AND BONUS MATERIALS

Additional Practices and Activities Not Listed Above

Take a bubble bath
Go for a walk around the block
Spray yourself with rosewater
Use aromatherapy

Give yourself a foot rub
Practice yoga or stretch
Practice an entire form of Sheng Zhen (see Resources for videos)
Call up a friend
Take yourself out on a date
Sex
Read
Pull weeds or tend to houseplants or garden

Add your own in the blank space below:

Appendix 2

HEALTHY SNACKS
AND SHOPPING LIST

Filling up on sensory stimulation and orgasmic energy will help plenty, but of course you also do need to eat. So I've listed some healthy snacks and a shopping list of foods to have on hand.

Healthy Snacks:

- Agar agar made with fruit juice, tea or chocolate or carob milk (dairy or dairy-free)
- Almonds or cashew butter
- Apples or raspberries and cheese if eating dairy and fruit
- Avocado and pink Himalayan salt on toast, rice cakes, or crackers
- Shredded beets and carrots
- Carob Maca Pumpkin Seed Milk: Blend 1 cup water with ¼ cup raw shelled pumpkin seeds in a high speed blender with a few ice cubes, 1 tbsp. of maca, and 2 tbsp. of raw carob powder (optional: add a couple drops of SweetLeaf Whole Leaf Stevia and/or 1-2 tbsp. of Organic Gemini's Tigernut Smoothie Mix)
- Celery
- Chia seed pudding

- Corn tortillas (sprouted): Warm or toasted until crisp with lemon or lime and sea salt
- Medjool dates with almond or cashew butter
- Nut butter on unsalted rice cake or rye bread; add your own sea salt. Optional: add honey or coconut nectar if eating sweeteners
- Oats (toasted) with flax oil, stevia, and carob
- Olives
- Pumpkin seeds

Shopping List:

- Avocado
- Bananas
- Beets
- Broth (mushroom, veggie, or bone or make your own)
- Brown rice
- Carob powder (raw)
- Carrots
- Celery
- Chia seeds or chia seed pudding (Chia Pods by The Chia Co)
- Chlorella
- Coconut oil
- Corn tortillas (Food for Life's Sprouted Corn Tortillas)
- Cucumbers
- Dates
- Dulse (or nori)
- Eggs
- Figs
- Flax seeds and/or flax oil

- Garlic
- Ginger root
- Golden berries (Navitas Naturals or bulk)
- Hummus
- Leafy greens (kale, arugula, spinach)
- Lemons (for lemon water in the morning)
- Luna & Larry's Coconut Bliss (for an ice cream substitute)
- Mushrooms (portobello, shitake)
- Nuts (almonds, cashews, walnuts)
- Oats
- Oat milk
- Olives
- Olive oil
- Peas (frozen or fresh)
- Popcorn
- Pumpkin seeds
- Quinoa
- Salt (Celtic sea salt or Himalayan pink)
- Stevia (SweetLeaf's Whole Leaf Stevia)
- Stevia-sweetened chocolate (Lily's or Coco Polo)
- Sugar snap peas
- Tea (herbal non-caffeinated or green)
- Tigernut Smoothie Mix (Organic Gemini)
- … and anything mentioned in the Healthy Snacks List or Aphrodisiacs that's not listed here!

Appendix 3

STARTING A
MULTI-ORGASMIC DIET
BOOK CLUB OR MEETUP GROUP

When we come together with like-minded women, we inspire and support one another by sharing our joys, our struggles, our laughter, our tears, and our wisdom. You absolutely can have great success using the Multi-Orgasmic Diet on your own. But if you'd like to gather with other women, this is how I suggest organizing your time together, whether it's through www.meetup.com or by starting a book club.

1. For each meeting, focus on only one chapter or less. You can meet weekly, every other week, or even monthly if you really want to take your time with it.

2. Begin your time with one another by agreeing upon confidentiality and then introducing yourselves and sharing your intentions with the group. Set a timer with a pleasant ring tone (i.e., chimes) for two to five minutes per woman.

3. Next, if you're comfortable leading a meditation or guided relaxation, do so. Or use one of the guided meditations in the book bonuses or simply instruct everyone to shut their eyes, relax their bodies, and focus on their breath (with or without some soft music playing). I recommend five to ten minutes for this.

4. After meditation, begin some discussion around questions posed by the book or questions you formulate on your own in preparation for facilitating the group. You can have this be a more

informal discussion where women freely talk back and forth with one another, or you can give each woman two to five minutes to share her thoughts without interruption or commenting regarding her share. How you do this might depend on whether it's a book club or a Meetup group. It's up to you and the women who would like to participate.

5. Take some time to explore at least one of the practices from the book in this group setting. The practice will influence the length of time needed.

6. Bring your meeting to a formal close with a round of check-ins about the practice. Again, two to five minutes is usually plenty of time for this.

7. Optional: unstructured social time.

About the Author

Rebecca Clio Gould is a Women's Holistic Health & Empowerment Coach specializing in spirituality and sexuality. She graduated from the Institute for Integrative Nutrition as a certified Integrative Nutrition Health Coach and is also a certified Sheng Zhen Teacher, Supreme Science Qigong Instructor, and Sexual Awakening for Women Facilitator. Rebecca began studying and practicing energywork in 1996, after a nearly fatal car accident, and has been a Board Certified Holistic Health Practitioner since 2007. She has extensive training in various modalities and has studied with some of the best teachers in her fields, including Paul Pitchford, Shakti Malan, and Master Li Junfeng.

Rebecca's mission is to help women step into their power and joy by opening their hearts and by breaking free from the illusory, self-imposed, and society-induced limitations that have been keeping them from blossoming into their full potential. She teaches that it's time for liberation, to truly enjoy and live life—emotionally, physically and sexually—to the fullest. Rebecca is known for her grounded spirituality, playful spirit, and calm demeanor as well as the effective techniques she shares.

Rebecca lives in Seattle, Washington. And when she is not writing or working, you are most likely to find her out in nature or on the dance floor—or just enjoying some down time, relaxing at home or trying her best not to kill her plants (a.k.a. learning how to garden). She also enjoys painting, singing in her car, and spending quality time with her family and friends.

To contact Rebecca, please visit www.rebeccacliogould.com.